CHOOSE YOUR ATTITUDES, CHANGE YOUR LIFE

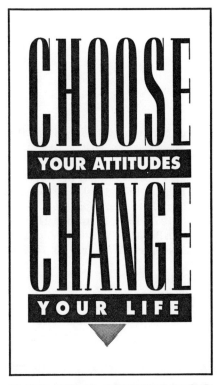

CHOOSE
YOUR ATTITUDES
CHANGE
YOUR LIFE

ROBERT JEFFRESS

VICTOR BOOKS®
A DIVISION OF SCRIPTURE PRESS PUBLICATIONS INC.
USA CANADA ENGLAND

Copy Editor: James R. Adair
Cover Design: Mardelle Ayres
Cover Photo: West Stock, Matt Brown

Library of Congress Cataloging-in-Publication Data

Jeffress, Robert, 1955-
    Choose your attitudes, change your life / by Robert Jeffress.
       p.   cm.
    Includes bibliographical references.
    ISBN 0-89693-123-4
    1. Christian life — 1960- 2. Attitude (Psychology) — Religious aspects — Christianity. I. Title.
    BV4501.2.J39   1992
    248.4 — dc20   91-38340
                                                CIP

---

1 2 3 4 5 6 7 8 9 10 Printing/Year 96 95 94 93 92

CONTENTS

Dedicated to my grandparents,
Robert E.B. Fielder and Dorothy U.T. Fielder,
whose lives have been
living illustrations of the positive attitudes
described in this book.

Newly drafted NFL players from the inner city rarely remain in the two-room hovels where they were raised. A person cured of inoperable cancer rarely sees life the same way as before. It is nearly impossible to find a butterfly that still crawls in the dirt and wiggles up trunks of vines to eat leaves. Yet Christians who have their basic nature radically changed by conversion and have no visible change in their behavior are a dime a dozen.

Why are so many who are so radically changed acting so completely the same?

Robert Jeffress tackles this problem head-on with practical steps that can help each of us begin to see the intended results of what God has already done within us. In the midst of a deluge of books that place more information in our heads, it is refreshing to see a book directed to help us apply the information already there and growing moldy from lack of use.

Choose Your Attitudes, Change Your Life is not the typical positive thinking book that is sweet to eat, quick to swallow, but not much to satisfy hunger. Robert Jeffress has done an excellent job of presenting deep biblical truths in a message of hope. His step-by-step approach to illustrate and to apply biblical truths brings the insight of a scholar down to the level of those of us who are interested in bottom-line results and a real life change.

Dr. Howard G. Hendricks
Chairman, Center for Christian Leadership
Distinguished Professor, Dallas Theological Seminary

CHAPTER ONE

ATTITUDE IS EVERYTHING

*"And do not be conformed
to this world, but be transformed by the renewing of
your mind, that you may
prove what the will of God
is, that which is good and
acceptable and perfect."*
Rom. 12:2

■ The surgeon was using unfamiliar terms. Yet, as he described my father's cancer and all of the possible scenarios
for the months that lay ahead, the doctor made a comment
that I will never forget: *"Attitude is everything."*

What an amazing statement! With all the medical tech-
nology available for a patient's prognosis, the doctor was
saying there is a variable that cannot be measured, and yet
could have the most profound impact on a person's longevity—the patient's attitude.

I immediately thought of philosopher William James'
comment: "Perhaps the greatest discovery of this century
is that if you can change your attitude, you can change
your life."

A changed life is the bottom line of Christianity and attitude is the key to this change. Theologians talk about three
types of changes that occur in a Christian's life: a positional
change, a progressive change, and a permanent change.

The positional change occurs the moment we trust in Jesus Christ for the forgiveness of our sins. The Bible says at the moment we make that decision we have "passed out of death into life" (1 John 3:14). The technical term for that positional change is "justification." Justification is a legal term that describes a change in our standing before God. Such a change is completed the moment we trust Christ. A person cannot be anymore justified than he was the moment he became a Christian.

There is also a permanent change awaiting Christians beyond the grave—"glorification." That term describes the exchange of our old bodies for new bodies—bodies free from disease, decay, and death. Paul talks about that future change in 1 Corinthians 15:50-52:

> Now I say this, brethren, that flesh and blood cannot inherit the kingdom of God; nor does the perishable inherit the imperishable. Behold, I tell you a mystery; we shall not all sleep, but we shall all be changed, in a moment, in the twinkling of an eye, at the last trumpet; for the trumpet will sound, and the dead will be raised imperishable, and we shall be changed.

But there is also a change that should be occurring in every Christian's life right now. It is a progressive change that begins the moment one becomes a Christian and continues until the day he dies. God is in the business of changing Christians to become just like Jesus Christ in character: "For whom He foreknew, He also predestined to become conformed to the image of His Son, that He might be the first-born among many brethren" (Rom. 8:29). The verse that immediately precedes this verse is one of the most-loved and oft-quoted passages in the Bible: "And we know that God causes all things to work together for good to those who love God, to those who are called according to His purpose."

Yes, God does work all things together for good. But what is "good"? And what about the qualifying phrase "to those who are called according to His purpose"? Verse 29 answers both of those questions. God's idea of "good" is to use every circumstance in your life to mold you into the image of His Son. How much difference is there between your character and the character of Jesus Christ? The answer to that question will give you a clue as to how much change you can expect in your life!

God's sovereign purpose is to change us into the image of His Son. Yet, we can choose whether or not we will cooperate with God in that process. We can choose to allow life circumstances either to strengthen us or to destroy us. The determining factor is our *attitude*. Here is a good definition of attitude: *Attitude is our mental and emotional response to the circumstances of life.*

We may not be able to change many of our circumstances, but we can change our attitudes. And remember William James' words, "If you can change your attitude, you can change your life."

What are these life-changing attitude choices we must make? My study of God's Word, coupled with my own experience as a pastor, reveals eleven essential attitude choices we must all make to experience the transformed life God intends for each of us. I have listed these attitudes in the form of eleven resolutions:

☐ I will choose purpose over aimlessness.
☐ I will choose perseverance over defeat.
☐ I will choose faith over worry.
☐ I will choose repentance over guilt.
☐ I will choose relaxation over stress.
☐ I will choose contentment over comparison.
☐ I will choose forgiveness over bitterness.
☐ I will choose productivity over slothfulness.
☐ I will choose humility over pride.
☐ I will choose companionship over loneliness.
☐ I will choose intimacy with God over isolation.

Now, before you close the book at this point and say, "I knew it, another one of those 'name it and claim it' positive thinking books," consider my frame of reference for this book. I realize that the eleven "I will" statements might sound to some disturbingly similar to Lucifer's five "I will" statements recorded in Isaiah 14:13-14. I am aware of such books as *The Seduction of Christianity* which totally repudiate the self-help philosophies of our day. And I am sympathetic with the skepticism of many evangelical Christians toward this whole emphasis on positive thinking.

But I fear we may have thrown the proverbial baby out with the bath water. Yes, man is totally depraved and capable of no good thing—apart from Jesus Christ. But those Christians who are utterly opposed to the positive-thinking movement forget a very simple principle found in 2 Corinthians 5:17: "Therefore if any man is in Christ, he is a new creature; the old things are passed away; behold new things have come."

While the non-Christian does not have the spiritual resources necessary to fully implement the eleven resolutions, the Christian has the unlimited power of the Holy Spirit to aid him. The Apostle Paul undoubtedly had this in mind when he said, "I can do all things through Him who strengthens me" (Phil. 4:13).

I believe that you can emphasize the importance of positive attitudes and actions without falling into humanism. One does not have to turn to Robert Schuller and Norman Vincent Peale to see the value of positive attitudes. The Bible is full of exhortations to choose the right attitudes. Why? Because our attitudes ultimately determine our actions. Consider some Bible passages related to the importance of right thinking (italics mine):

And it is he who will go as a forerunner before Him in the spirit and power of Elijah, to turn the hearts of the fathers back to the children, and the disobedient to the *attitude* of the righteous, so as to make ready a people prepared for the Lord (Luke 1:17).

For the *mind* set on the flesh is death, but the *mind* set on the Spirit is life and peace (Rom. 8:6).

And do not be conformed to this world, but be transformed by the *renewing of your mind* . . . (Rom. 12:2).

Be of the same *mind* toward one another; do not be haughty in *mind* . . . (Rom. 12:16).

Lay aside the old self, which is being corrupted in accordance with the lusts of deceit, and that you be *renewed in the spirit of your mind* (Eph. 4:22-23).

Have this *attitude* in yourselves which was also in Christ Jesus (Phil. 2:5).

Let us therefore, as many as are perfect, have this *attitude;* and if in anything you have a different *attitude,* God will reveal that also to you (Phil. 3:15).

Finally, brethren, whatever is true, whatever is honorable, whatever is right, whatever is pure, whatever is lovely, whatever is of good repute, if there is any excellence and if anything worthy of praise, *let your mind dwell on these things* (Phil. 4:8).

To neglect the importance of attitudes in life is to be totally unbiblical!

Before we examine each of these eleven critical attitudes, there are five basic principles about attitudes that are foundational to our understanding:

1. Our attitudes are chosen. We can choose to look at any situation positively or negatively. Tim Hansel retells the following story in his book *Eating Problems for Breakfast:*

There were two farmers. One was a pessimist and the other was an optimist. When the sun was shining, the optimist would say, "Wonderful sunshine," but the pessimist would respond, "Yeah, but I'm afraid it's going to scorch the crops." When it rained, the optimist would say, "Fine rain," but the pessimist would respond, "Yeah, but I'm afraid we're going to have a flood."

One day the optimist said to the pessimist, "Have you seen my new bird dog? He's the finest money can buy." The pessimist said, "You mean that little mutt I saw penned up behind your house? He don't look like much to me." The optimist said, "Well, how about going hunting with me tomorrow?" The pessimist agreed.

They went and shot some ducks. The ducks landed in the pond. The optimist ordered his dog to go get the ducks. The dog obediently responded, but instead of swimming in the water, the dog walked on top of the water, retrieved the ducks, and then walked back on top of the water. The optimist now turned confidently to his pessimist friend, hoping that this would have impressed him. The determined pessimist replied, "Hmm . . . can't swim, can he?"[1]

Some people are confirmed pessimists! They make a deliberate decision to have a negative mental and emotional response to every circumstance. Yet other people can look at the same circumstances and choose a positive outlook. The Apostle Paul is a good example of one who chose to have a positive attitude, regardless of his circumstances.

The Epistle to the Philippians has much to say about right attitudes. When you understand Paul's circumstances when he penned these words, you can better appreciate his optimistic attitude. Paul was not sunbathing on the Riviera, sipping a cool drink, while he wrote, "Rejoice in the Lord, always." Instead, he was in a Roman prison, awaiting his possible execution. Yet Paul was able to say, "I have learned to be content in whatever circumstances I am" (Phil. 4:11). We will discover his secret for such a positive attitude in the next chapter.

In their excellent book on depression, *Happiness Is a Choice*, Drs. Frank Minirth and Paul Meier remind us that our emotions are determined by choices we make:

The Christian who is depressed is depressed because he is choosing (either out of ignorance of the Word or else on purpose) to be depressed, choosing not to live by God's principles. Living by God's principles results in the fruits of the Spirit. . . .[2]

2. Our attitudes are influenced by input. To a large extent, our attitudes are shaped by external influences: what we read, what we watch, who we listen to, and what we think about. The primary counseling problem I encounter as a pastor is depression. I am amazed at the number of depressed individuals I deal with who openly admit they are addicted to soap operas. No wonder they are depressed! Yes, maybe it is an overused analogy, but it is accurate—the mind is like a computer. Garbage in, garbage out. That is why Paul wrote:

Whatever is true, whatever is honorable, whatever is right, whatever is pure, whatever is lovely, whatever is of good repute, if there is any excellence and if anything worthy of praise, let your mind dwell on these things (Phil. 4:8).

Attitudes are not only influenced by what we read and watch but also by our friends. Luke 1:17 speaks of "the attitude of the righteous" in contrast to the attitude of the ungodly. What a contrast there is between the attitudes of the godly and the attitudes of the ungodly! That is why the Book of Proverbs is full of warnings about avoiding certain types of people. Solomon's father, David, also warned his readers to avoid relationships with the ungodly:

How blessed is the man who does not walk in the counsel of the wicked, nor stand in the path of sinners, nor sit in the seat of scoffers! But his delight is in the law of the Lord, and in His law he meditates day and night (Ps. 1:1-2).

Solomon and David both understood that attitudes are highly contagious.

3. Our attitudes affect our relationships. All of us are involved in relationships that could stand improvement— relationships with our spouses, our children, our friends, our work associates, or our fellow church members. Did you know that the Bible teaches that a wrong attitude is the major source of relationship conflicts? For example, James 4:1:

> What is the source of quarrels and conflicts among you? Is not the source your pleasures that wage war in your members?

The major source of conflicts is a selfish attitude. Whenever you get two or more people together who are determined to get their way, you are going to have conflict, whether it is in the home, at work, or in the church. What is the solution to such conflict? Again, the answer is attitude.

> Do not merely look out for your own personal interests, but also for the interests of others. Have this *attitude* in yourselves which was also in Christ Jesus, who, although He existed in the form of God, did not regard equality with God a thing to be grasped, but emptied Himself (Phil. 2:4-7).

4. Our attitudes are both the cause and the result of right behavior. It is easy to see how right thinking produces right behavior. This book is built upon that foundational premise. And such a premise is biblical: "As [man] thinketh in his heart, so is he" (Prov. 23:7, KJV). But it is also true that right actions also produce right attitudes.

Remember the story of Cain and Abel? Cain was despondent because his brother, Abel, had offered an acceptable sacrifice to God, whereas Cain's gift had been rejected. What did God prescribe as a cure for Cain's depression? Look at Genesis 4:6-7: "Then the Lord said to Cain, 'Why are you angry? And why has your countenance fallen? If you do well, will not your countenance be lifted up? And if you do not do well, sin is crouching at the door; and its desire is for you, but you must master it.' " God said that if Cain would *do* right, he would start to *feel* right. Right actions produce right attitudes.

How different that is from our mind-set today. We live in a feeling-oriented society: "If it feels good, do it" (and the corollary, "If it doesn't feel good, don't do it!). A husband or wife seeks a divorce because he or she "doesn't feel anything any longer." People quit their jobs because they "don't feel fulfilled." Christians quit going to church because they "don't feel the Spirit" in the services. Yet, God's word to Cain was that the key to right feelings is right actions.

When people say to me, "Robert, I feel so 'blah' about my faith. I've lost the excitement I once felt," I immediately ask them about their spiritual disciplines. Are they reading God's Word daily? How much time are they spending in prayer? When is the last time they led someone to Christ? The usual reply is, "I just don't *feel* motivated to do those things." I always have the same response: "If you wait until you feel like it, you'll never do it! Do those things out of obedience to God, and eventually you will recover those lost feelings."

5. Our attitude determines our destiny. Attitudes profoundly impact life, death, and even eternity. Psychologist Dennis Waitley illustrates how attitudes affect life in his book *Seeds of Greatness*. In this book, he relates his study of returning POWs from Viet Nam.

The POWs and hostages who seemed to be in the best physical and emotional condition after their ordeal were the ones who had used the seven years, in some cases, or the 444 days, in others, as a "university without walls.". . . There were no books—nothing to read, nothing to write with, or paint with, or look at, just the walls. The only light was artificial and that always seemed to be on . . . the glaring bulb causes disorientation, fatigue, and distress, precisely the responses desired by the prison guards, terrorists, and cult leaders to make their captives more susceptible to their wills. . . . In the absence of any materials, tools, or comforts, they simply created them in their imaginations. They recalled most of the inspirational events and significant learning stored in their memories. . . . Some of the POWs reconstructed well-known passages from the Bible, which became their source of inner strength. Some played golf, by replaying games from memory at their favorite golf courses in previous years. When they tired of replaying old games, they started preplaying future tournaments with their favorite PGA pro.[3]

Our attitudes cannot only lengthen our lives, as Waitely demonstrated, but they can also shorten our lives. In his book *Head First: The Biology of Hope*, Norman Cousins observed that the brain is the most prolific gland in the human body, capable of activating both healing secretions, and deadly poisons in our body—according to our attitudes.

But the most convincing argument for right attitudes is the effect they have on our eternity. Remember the definition of an attitude—*"our mental or emotional response to the circumstances of life."* While we all experience many varied circumstances in life, there is one common circumstance we all encounter: sin. Sin is our failure to please God. And the Bible says all of us are guilty of it. What is your attitude toward that failure in your life? Your attitude will affect where you spend eternity.

Some face that reality with an attitude of unbelief—there is no God, and there is no such thing as sin. Some face sin with an attitude of indifference—so what? Others face that reality with an attitude of pride—I may not be perfect, but I'm better than most people. But there is only one attitude that pleases God: an attitude of repentance. That means agreeing with God that you have failed, and turning to Him for forgiveness. The Apostle John wrote, "If we confess our sins, He is faithful and righteous to forgive us our sins and to cleanse us from all unrighteousness" (1 John 1:9).

Perhaps, then, an improvement on William James' statment would read: "Perhaps the greatest discovery of this century is that if you can change your attitude, you can change your life *and your eternal destiny!*"

CHAPTER TWO

CHOOSING PURPOSE OVER AIMLESSNESS

*"Live life, then, with a due
sense of responsibility, not
as men who do not know the
meaning and purpose of
life, but as those who do.
Make the best use of your
time, despite all the evils of
these days. Don't be vague,
but grasp firmly what you
know to be the will of the
Lord."   Eph. 5:15-17, PH*

■ Thomas Chalmers once said, "The grand essentials of happiness are: something to do, something to love, and something to hope for." Put another way, the key to happiness in life is to have a clearly defined purpose for living. Purpose in life is the foundation on which we build our actions, our affections, and our aspirations. Someone has said that purpose is the engine that drives our lives. And yet, it is amazing how few people have a clearly defined life purpose. Studies show that less than 3 percent of Americans have clearly defined life goals. No wonder the past decade was known as "the aimless eighties."

The premise of this book is that right attitudes are the keys to happiness in life. Each of the eleven attitudes explored in this book are nonoptional for successful living.

Certainly, a strong case could be built for the preeminence of each of these attitudes. Yet, I am convinced that purpose has to rank at the top of the list in importance. Without purpose, we are condemned to live lives of quiet desperation, as Thoreau said.

Charles Colson clearly illustrates the need for purpose in life in his book *Kingdoms in Conflict*. Colson recounts the story of a group of Jewish prisoners in a Nazi concentration camp who suddenly found that the factory building where they had been working had been bombed by allied aircraft.

The next morning several hundred inmates were herded to one end of its charred remains. Expecting orders to begin rebuilding, they were startled when the Nazi officer commanded them to shovel sand into carts and drag it to the other end of the plant.

The next day the process was repeated in reverse; they were ordered to move the huge pile of sand back to the other end of the compound. A mistake has been made, they thought. Stupid swine. Day after day they hauled the same pile of sand from one end of the camp to the other. Then Dostoyevski's prediction came true. One old man began crying uncontrollably; the guards hauled him away. Another screamed until he was beaten into silence. Then a young man who had survived three years in the camp darted away from the group. The guards shouted for him to stop as he ran toward the electrified fence. The other prisoners cried out, but it was too late; there was a blinding flash and a terrible sizzling noise as smoke puffed from his smoldering flesh. In the days that followed, dozens of prisoners went mad and ran from their work, only to be shot by the guards or electrocuted by the fence. The commandant smugly remarked that there soon would be "no more need to use the crematoria." The gruesome lesson is plain: men will cling to life with dogged resolve while working meaningfully, even if that work supports their hated captors. But purposeless labor soon snaps the mind.[1]

What was true in a Nazi concentration camp is true to-day. Purposeless labor soon snaps the mind.

■ *Defining Purpose*

What do we mean when we talk about "purpose?" To understand this attitude, we must differentiate between a "purpose," and "objective," and a "goal."

A purpose is a statement that answers the question, "Why do I exist?" Such a statement does not need to be a lengthy treatise, but it can be a simple sentence stating a person's reason for living. Organizations should have a purpose, and individuals should have a purpose.

An organization that cannot clearly express its purpose will find itself in continual turmoil. The General Motors Corporation might say that its purpose is "to generate a healthy profit by manufacturing the finest cars in the world." Every objective and goal of GM should in some way contribute to that broad purpose.

Such a statement is broad, and yet it gives direction to the company. It keeps the company's activities focused. A GM vice-president might come to the president one day and say, "You know, I've been thinking; there seems to be a lot of money to be made in pharmaceuticals. I think we ought to explore that option." The only problem is that such a venture does not mesh with the overall purpose of the company — "manufacturing the finest cars in America." Although a purpose statement can be changed, it is usually continuous.

A church might model its purpose statement after the Great Commission: "Our reason for existing is to win people to Jesus Christ and help them mature in their faith." Having adopted such a purpose statement means that every program of the church should either be designed for evangelism (winning people to Christ) or for edification (helping them mature in their faith). Such a purpose statement would also prevent the church from engaging in a number of activities, such as operating a clinic for the poor, teaching a seminar on real-estate investing, or sponsoring Monday night bingo.

Individuals also need to formulate purpose statements to

guide their lives. A good purpose statement should cover twenty years or more of a person's life. A purpose statement is usually broad and cannot be measured. But it is useful in giving general direction to a person's life. Here are some examples of purpose statements that an individual might adopt:

"TO BE A MODEL PARENT FOR MY CHILDREN."
"TO ENJOY LIFE TO THE FULLEST EXTENT POSSIBLE."
"TO BE WEALTHY."
"TO GIVE GLORY TO GOD ALL OF MY LIFE."

Someone has said that every life exists either to meet a need or to fill a greed. Notice that in the above examples, two of those purpose statements are designed to meet a need; the other two are designed to fill a greed. Hopefully, your purpose statement—the guiding beacon of your life—will be built around meeting a need.

God has given you both the desire and the ability to fulfill a unique need in His world. And you are the only person who is capable of meeting that unique need! Lest you be tempted to think that this is just some more of that positive-thinking jargon, look at what the Word of God says: "For it is God who is at work within you, giving you the will and the power to achieve His purpose (Phil. 2:13, PH).

Everyone of us is aware of certain needs in our society. Such an awareness does not come on our own, according to the Apostle Paul. God is the one who gives us that desire. Why? So that we might achieve His purpose.

For example, here is a businessperson who is concerned about the inability of Christians to integrate their Christianity with their work. So he devotes his life to being a model of a Christian businessperson and teaching others the principles he has learned. Or here is a mother who is distressed about drunk drivers because of a tragedy in her own life. So she devotes her life to battling the menace of drunk drivers in our society. Or here is a preacher who is concerned that traditional church services are not reaching unbelievers. So he devotes his life to developing a church that will appeal to the person who knows nothing about Christianity. All of these are real examples of people who found God's purpose in their lives by trying to meet a need of particular concern to them.

What needs do you see that move you? What makes you angry? What causes you to lie awake some nights? The answer to these questions will help you discover your purpose in life. Bobb Biehl, president of Masterplanning Group International, suggests six questions to assist you in identifying the needs about which you feel most passionate. Take some time to answer the following questions:

1. What needs do you see in the world that concern you?

2. If I could meet any need in the world, what need would I meet?

3. What are the most urgent needs in my country, my community, my work, my school, and my church?

4. What age group or type of people naturally interests me?

5. What are the major needs among my neighbors, my friends, and my family?

6. If I do not meet these needs, who will?[2]

■ *Formulating a Purpose Statement*
As you examine those needs that most concern you, it might be difficult to identify which need should guide your life purpose. How do you know which need you should spend your life trying to fulfill? Obviously, it should be a

need that passionately concerns you. But it also should be a need that you are qualified to meet. For example, I can work up a lot of emotion over the need to find a cure for AIDS. Certainly, I could make a legitimate case for a purpose statement that would say, "My reason for existing is . . . to find a cure for AIDS." Such a purpose statement is obviously built around "meeting a need" rather than "filling a greed." However, there is one small problem with my adopting that purpose statement. *I have no gifts or interest in science.* I almost failed biology because of my inability to ever see *anything* through a microscope. How in the world could I ever expect to find the cure for AIDS?

A legitimate life purpose should be built around both needs that strongly concern you AND gifts that you possess. Look again at Philippians 2:13. "For it is God who is at work within you, giving you the will *and the power* to achieve His purpose" (PH, italics mine).

If God intends for you to meet a particular need, He will give you the unique abilities necessary to meet that challenge. Several years ago, I formulated this purpose statement: "My purpose in life is to communicate God's message effectively."

I have a burning desire to communicate God's Word in a clear, interesting, and practical way. Preachers who bore people with biblical truth disturb me, as do Bible teachers who seem to have a "gift" for making the abstract truths of Scripture even more abstract. Through my preaching, teaching, and writing ministries, I want to help people understand the exciting and life-changing truths of the Bible.

Yet suppose I had no gifts whatsoever in communication. Suppose I stuttered and stammered in front of crowds and could not write a simple sentence. Obviously, I would not be a very effective communicator and should consider another life purpose.

Now I know some of you Bible students out there are thinking, "Wait a minute, what about Moses? He stuttered and stammered, yet God gave him the supernatural ability to communicate." Yes, that's true. But Moses' major purpose in life was not to be an effective communicator but to be a leader of God's people. And throughout Moses' life, beginning in Pharoah's palace, he demonstrated a natural ability to lead.

My point is simply this: Before you seek to develop your life purpose statement, have a clear understanding of the gifts and abilities God has given you. God will use you to fill a need for which He has already gifted you. To try to identify those gifts you might have, take a moment to answer the following questions:

1. What abilities do you have that other people seem to notice and appreciate?

2. Suppose you were asked to give a "How To" seminar in your church or civic group on any topic you chose. What topic would you feel most comfortable addressing?

3. Outside of recreational pursuits, list five accomplishments that have given you the most satisfaction. What aspect of these experiences did you enjoy?

4. Is there a common denominator that you find in all or most of the above experiences? What is it?

5. Hopefully, these questions have helped you identify one area in which you are both interested and gifted. In a word, what is that area?

Now that you have identified both the needs that concern you and the gifts God has given you, see if you can write a sentence that describes your life purpose.

My purpose in life is to:

Some purpose statements will be very specific:

My purpose in life is to be a model father to my children and to encourage other men to do the same.

Other purpose statements may be broader:

My purpose in life is to glorify God all the days of my life.

But whether the purpose is broad or specific, it should have a spiritual dimension. What do I mean by that? Simply that we should ask for God's leadership in discovering the unique reason He has placed us on this planet. In John 4:34, Jesus gave one of these simple purpose statements: "My food [purpose] is to do the will of Him who sent Me, and to accomplish His work" (John 4:34).

■ *Objectives*

In order for us to realize our life purposes, it is important for us to be able to connect our life purpose to the major components of our everyday life. A purpose to "glorify God all the days of my life" is noble. But how does that purpose affect my friendships, my profession, my family, or my finances? That is where objectives come in. Objectives are simple statements expressing our desires for specific areas of our lives. Take a moment to examine the seven major areas of your life. On a scale of 1-10, how would you evaluate the following areas of your life?

1. Spiritual	1	2	3	4	5	6	7	8	9	10
2. Physical	1	2	3	4	5	6	7	8	9	10
3. Family	1	2	3	4	5	6	7	8	9	10
4. Vocational	1	2	3	4	5	6	7	8	9	10
5. Personal Growth	1	2	3	4	5	6	7	8	9	10
6. Social	1	2	3	4	5	6	7	8	9	10
7. Financial	1	2	3	4	5	6	7	8	9	10[3]

Most likely, you are pleased with several areas of your life. In those areas, your objective will be to continue doing what you are already doing. There are other areas that probably need improvement. While a purpose statement completes the sentence "My reason for living is to . . .," an objective statement completes the sentence "I want to . . ." or "I want to continue to . . ." for each of the seven major areas of life. Here is an example of an objective for each of the above areas:

    1. Spiritual: "I want to continue to grow in my relationship with God."
    2. Physical: "I want to live a long life."
    3. Family: "I want to spend more quality time with my family."
    4. Vocational: "I want to continue to progress in my career."
    5. Personal Growth: "I want to read more widely."
    6. Social: "I want to develop new friendships and keep in contact with significant friends from my past."
    7. Financial: "I want to have enough money to meet the needs of my family and to have a comfortable retirement."

Objectives help give direction to specific areas of our lives. Obviously, a person might have more than one objective for a certain area of life. For example, I have written three objectives for the physical area:

1. I want to live a long life.
2. I want to be free from serious illness.
3. I want to be more slender.

After spending some time examining the major areas of your life, jot down one or two objectives you have for each area:

Spiritual:

Physical:

Family:

Vocational:

Personal Growth:

Social:

Financial:

■ *Goals*

Goals are the vehicles by which we translate our objectives into reality. A goal is a desired accomplishment that is easily measured by time and performance. For example, my desire "to be more slender" is an objective. But a desire "to lose five pounds by Oct. 31" is a goal. Why? It is a stated objective that can be measured by time (Oct. 31) and by performance (five pounds).

When formulating goals, you should try to answer three questions:

1. What do I want to happen? (accomplishment)
2. How will I know it happened? (measurement) (Note: sometimes the measurement is a part of the accomplishment, i.e., "to lose five pounds")
3. When do I want this to happen? (starting date, or completion date)

To help you understand goals, let me give you a list of different goals I have seen others develop:

☐ I want to take my wife out to dinner twice a month, beginning March 1 *(Family)*.
☐ I want to save $1,000 by Dec. 31 *(Financial)*.

☐ I want to read a chapter of the Bible every day, beginning today *(Spiritual)*.

☐ I want to exercise at least twenty minutes a day, beginning today *(Physical)*.

☐ I want to read a book every month, beginning Feb. 1 *(Personal Growth)*.

☐ I want my business to grow ten percent by the end of the year *(Vocational)*.

☐ I want to call a friend each Saturday, beginning this week *(Social)*.

All of these goals state specific, measurable accomplishments. Notice how each of the goals contributes to my overall objectives in the seven major life areas. Now, after looking over the objectives you have established for those same areas, write down two goals for each area:

SPIRITUAL:
1.

2.

PHYSICAL:
1.

2.

FAMILY:
1.

2.

VOCATIONAL:
1.

2.

PERSONAL GROWTH:
1.

2.

SOCIAL:
1.

2.

FINANCIAL:
1.

2.

Now that you have a clearly defined life purpose, coupled with specific objectives and goals, you probably feel highly motivated. And that's good! By having carefully thought through a purpose statement, objectives, and goals you are ahead of 97 percent of the American population. Yet, sooner or later (probably sooner!) you are going to run into roadblocks to those goals that will seem insurmountable. That is why the next attitude we will discuss is essential if you are going to achieve your life purpose.

CHAPTER THREE

CHOOSING PERSEVERANCE OVER DEFEAT

*"I press on toward the goal
for the prize of the upward
call of God in Christ
Jesus."*   *Phil. 3:14*

■ Tim Hansel has a great story in his book *Eating Problems for Breakfast,* concerning a conversation he had with a wilderness scout named Bernie:

Late one afternoon as the blue western sky was beginning to fade into oranges and grays, he got to talking about the different experiences of people on his trips who became lost in the wilderness. "I've had lots of people get lost up here," he said. I responded, "That's probably because they don't really understand a map and compass all that well. Right?"

"Nope," he said.

"Well, it's probably because they are new to the wilderness," I said.

Again he replied, "Nope."

"Then it's probably because they are city folk and don't know east from west," I said.

"Nope," he replied.

"Well, is it because they are out here for the first time and they are rookies and stuff?" I asked.

"Nope," he said.

"Then it's because they don't understand the terrain." I said.

"Nope," he said.

"I must have asked him at least a dozen more questions to which I kept getting the same simple answer, "Nope." My curiosity finally won out, and I said, "Well then, how come they get lost all the time?"

"It's 'cause they don't go fer enuf!" he said. "I tell them to go five miles, and they go about three-fourths of a mile and start turning left and right and end up all over the place."[1]

Certainly, there are some people who get lost in life because they never have formulated a life purpose, accompanied by specific objectives and goals. Such people are like the rich Texan at the airline counter who said to the reservations clerk, "Lady, I want a first-class ticket."

"Where to, sir?" the clerk asked.

"It really don't matter," the Texan replied. "I've got business *everywhere!*"

A recent book title summed up the best reason for having goals—*If You Don't Know Where You Are Going, You Will Probably End Up Somewhere Else.*

Yet there are many other people, like the tourists in Hansel's story, who know where they want to go; they have directions on how to get there; but they give up before reaching their destination. They "don't go fer enuf." Such people end up just as lost as those who never had a destination in mind from the start.

In the last chapter, we talked about the importance of developing a life purpose and setting concrete objectives and goals to help achieve that grand purpose. Hopefully, you have set a number of goals and objectives for the seven major areas of your life. I imagine that you felt extremely motivated after writing down your desired accomplishments. Yet such enthusiasm will be short-lived unless you choose to adopt the attitude of perseverance.

What is perseverance? Someone has said that courage is the desire to begin something, but perseverance is the desire to continue. Perseverance is the attitude that says, "I will not give up, regardless of the obstacles I encounter."

During the dark days of Hitler's rise to power, Winston Churchill had the formidable task of holding his country together. Despite the continued attacks of the Germans, Churchill refused to surrender to or even to negotiate with the Nazis. On more than one occasion, Churchill's advisors and friends suggested that the prime minister might consider surrender or negotiation. But Churchill had a different philosophy about how to win. His simple motto was this: "Wars are not won by evacuations!"

Life is not won by evacuation, either. No matter what goals you have established for each area of life, sooner or later (probably sooner) you are going to be bombarded by obstacles. The measure of your success in achieving your goals will be your response to those obstacles. For the most part, you will not be able to control the obstacles, but you can control your response to those obstacles.

For example, suppose you have set a goal to save $300 a month, beginning this month. Your objective in setting that goal is to provide for the needs of your family and to enjoy a comfortable retirement—certainly a worthy objective. Let me tell you (from firsthand experience!) what is sure to happen. You will probably encounter some unusual expense that month that will keep you from saving $300. The car will break down, the washing machine will go out, or you will need to reshingle the roof.

Financial counseling books say you should "pay yourself first every month." In other words, put that $300 aside first, before you pay *any* other bills. While that sounds good, it simply doesn't always work. There are some financial obligations that arise that *cannot* be ignored. Try telling the IRS that you can't make your quarterly tax payment this quarter because you need to "pay yourself first."

Or let's say you have established a physical goal to exercise twenty minutes a day, beginning next Monday. Next Monday arrives and you are sick with the flu. Obviously, your natural response is to think, "So much for trying to exercise!" And for the next six months you go without any kind of regular exercise until you read a book like this and start to feel guilty.

One more example. Suppose you have set a goal in your spiritual life to get up twenty minutes earlier to read a chapter of the Bible and pray, beginning tomorrow. The alarm clock sounds—you hit the snooze button without even thinking. When you finally do awaken, you resolve to do better the next morning. When the alarm goes off the next morning, you think to yourself, "I've got such a busy day today, I could really use the extra twenty minutes of sleep." You roll over again. After repeating this process for several days, you think, *It's impossible for me to ever gain blanket victory. I'll have to find another time to have my devotional.* Sure.

My point is that there will be obstacles (either external or internal) that will work to keep you from achieving your goals. But persistence is not necessarily your ability to overcome an obstacle, as much as it is your willingness to continue pursuing your goal, regardless of your temporary set-back. The persistent person is that one who says:

"All right, I wasn't able to save that money this month, but I am going to try again next month."

"I am sick right now and do need to rest, but just as soon as I am well, I will resume my exercise program."

"I am so determined to have a twenty-minute devotional every morning that I will move the alarm clock across the room so I have to get up!"

While we cannot always control life's obstacles, we *can* control our response to those obstacles. Persistence is not the ability to overcome obstacles; it is the willingness to continue, in spite of obstacles.

I love this example of persistence found in our nation's history:

When he was seven years old, his family was forced out of their home on a legal technicality, and he had to work to help support them.

At age 9, his mother died.

At 22 he lost his job as a store clerk. He wanted to go to law school, but lacked the education.

At 23, he went into debt to become a partner in a small store.

At 26, his business partner died, leaving him a huge debt that took years to repay.

At 28, after courting a girl for four years, he asked her to marry him. She said, "No."

At 37, on his third try, he was elected to Congress, but two years later, he failed to be reelected.

At 41, his four-year-old son died.

At 45, he ran for the Senate and lost.

At 47, he failed as the vice-presidential candidate.

At 49, he ran for the Senate again, and lost.

At 51, he was elected President of the United States. His name was Abraham Lincoln.[2]

■ *Biblical Basis for Persistence*

As previously emphasized, this is a book about biblical attitudes. You can find numerous books about positive attitudes—including perseverance. But such books are usually void of any biblical foundation. Is perseverance a desirable attitude for the Christian, or is it just one more of man's attempts to be self-sufficient instead of God-sufficient? Such a question needs to be carefully examined.

There are those who say, "Whatever the mind can conceive and believe, it can achieve." While such a statement might make a nice wall plaque, it neglects an important truth. Not every goal the mind conceives is necessarily one that should be pursued. Adolph Hitler could have easily had that motto hanging in his bunker! The Word of God tells us that we need to be wary of what comes from our heart: "The heart is more deceitful than all else and is desperately sick: who can understand it?" (Jer. 17:9)

That is why we need to make sure that our goals are worthy of pursuit. How do we do that? While there is no easy formula for determining whether a goal is God's will for your life, let me suggest several questions you should ask yourself about your goals:

1. Does your goal violate any principles in God's Word? If the answer is "yes," you can expect God to

place obstacles in your path that no amount of persistence will overcome.

2. Is your goal in keeping with God's purpose for your life? Several years ago, I decided to write a television script. It was a goal that I pursued with bulldog tenacity. After completing the script, I began the process of selling it. After a trip to Hollywood, I soon realized that, while such a goal was not immoral, it was not in keeping with God's purpose for my life. Yes, I could have persevered in the goal, and I might have achieved it. But such a goal was not in keeping with God's plan for my life. So I crossed that goal off my list.

3. How will the achievement of your goal bring honor to God? You should be able to articulate how every goal you set will honor God. For example, a goal to lose twenty pounds could ultimately result in a longer life in which to serve God. Or a goal to spend more time with your family could result in a stronger family, which certainly honors God.

Thus, when we talk about perseverance, we are going to assume that the goal you are pursuing is one that meets the above criteria. Otherwise, your goal should *not* be pursued; it should be abandoned!

■ *And the Walls Came Tumbling Down*

The story of Joshua and the walls of Jericho provides a good illustration of both the basis and the results of persistence. Joshua and his people had a goal of conquering the land of Canaan. Such an objective was in keeping with God's will for Israel. However, there was one obstacle—the city of Jericho—that stood between Israel and her goal. A large wall around the city appeared to render victory impossible.

But God had clearly stated His desire for Israel to conquer Jericho: "And the Lord said to Joshua, 'See, I have given Jericho into your hand, with its king and the valiant warriors' " (Josh. 6:2). God commanded Joshua and the people to march around the nine-acre city of Jericho once a day for six days. Then, on the seventh day, they were to march around the city seven times. On the seventh time around the city, the people were to shout, the priests were to blow the trumpet, and the wall would fall down. If they followed these instructions, Jericho would be theirs.

When I read this story, I am impressed with the persistence such obedience required. I am sure that by the third or fourth day the Israelites were tiring of the morning ritual of marching around the city. Not only was such an exercise tiring, it was embarrassing. Can you imagine the insults and ridicule the people of Jericho must have hurled down to the Israelites, as they watched the Israelites from their perch atop the wall?

Yet, the Israelites' faith that God would do what He had promised caused them to be persistent in their obedience. By the way, biblical faith is never a hope or a wish. Faith is not some positive emotion that we try to conjure up within ourselves. The Bible says that "faith is the assurance of things hoped for, the conviction of things not seen" (Heb. 11:1). Faith always requires a concrete object. Faith is the confidence that God will do what He said He will do.

■ *The Seventh Time's a Charm*

We find another illustration of biblical persistence in the story of Naaman, the army captain who suffered from leprosy. After asking the Prophet Elisha how he might be healed of his disease, the prophet gave this instruction: "Go and wash in the Jordan seven times, and your flesh shall be restored to you and you shall be clean" (2 Kings 5:10). Naaman's reaction to the instruction was understandable. He was *furious*. Why? He wanted an immediate cure for his problem. "Behold, I thought, 'He will surely come out to me, and stand and call on the name of the Lord his God, and wave his hand over the place and cure the leper' " (2 Kings 5:11).

Naaman is like many of us. We desire the easy road to success. When someone suggests that victory might not come immediately, we become resentful. And when we are told to engage in what seem to be meaningless activities to achieve our goals, we become angry.

For example, Joshua 1:8 tells us that one key to success

in life is meditating on God's Word. "This book of the law shall not depart from your mouth, but you shall meditate on it day and night, so that you may be careful to do according to all that is written in it; for then you will make your way prosperous, and then you will have success." How does reading and meditating on passages in a book that is thousands of years old help me be successful today? We may not be sure—much as Naaman was not sure how dipping himself in a muddy river would heal his leprosy. But God commanded him to do it. And in the same way, God has promised that persistence in meditating on His Word will bring success in life.

What was the result of Naaman's persistence in an activity that seemed to have little payoff? "So he went down and dipped himself seven times in the Jordan, according to the word of the man of God; and his flesh was restored like the flesh of a little child, and he was clean" (2 Kings 5:14). Notice that the first dip in the river did not cure Naaman. Nor did the second or third. I would imagine that by the fifth or sixth time Naaman was tempted to say, "This isn't working!" But his persistence in obeying Elisha's command finally paid off.

Let's review what we have learned about persistence:

1. We should persist only in those goals, objectives, and purposes that we have determined are God's will for our lives.

2. Persistence does not necessarily mean overcoming obstacles that keep us from achieving our goals; instead, persistence means continuing to pursue our objectives *in spite of* obstacles that come our way.

3. Persistence sometimes requires that we continue in activities that have little immediate value (remember Joshua and Naaman).

Now that we have established a biblical basis for cultivating the attitude of persistence, let's consider how to develop the attitude of persistence.

■ *Four Keys to Developing Persistence*
1. Understand the value of persistence. Many people are content with failure because deep down in their innermost

selves they do not feel they were ever destined for success. They feel that they do not possess the gifts necessary to achieve their wildest dreams. Yet, the truth is that people do not differ significantly in ability. In his book *The Range of Human Capacities*, psychologist Dr. David Wechsler says, "The differences that separate the masses of mankind from one another—with respect to any one or all of their capabilities—are small. As compared with other ratios or orders or differences in nature, they are pitifully insignificant."[3]

What, then, is the extra edge in life that separates the successful from the unsuccessful? It is the attitude of persistence. Napoleon Hill made that same observation after years of study of successful men and women: "I had the happy privilege of analyzing both Mr. Edison and Mr. Ford, year by year, over a long period of years, and therefore, the opportunity to study them at close range; so I speak from actual knowledge when I say that I found no quality save persistence, in either of them, that even remotely suggested the major source of their stupendous achievements."[4]

Some of my favorite words about the value of persistence came from President Calvin Coolidge:

Press on: Nothing in the world can take the place of persistence. Talent will not; nothing is more common than unsuccessful men with talent. Genius will not; unrewarded genius is almost a proverb. Education will not; the world is full of educated derelicts. Persistence and determination alone are overwhelmingly powerful.[5]

2. Anticipate obstacles in achieving your goals. One way to overcome obstacles in your pursuit of your goals is to anticipate them! I remember reading the story of the president of a major soft-drink manufacturer who asked his sales team to develop a new marketing strategy for a product. After team members made their presentation, the president asked them what obstacles they anticipated in achieving their goal. Silence. After a few moments, the president sent them back to the drawing board. He reasoned that their plan was not bold enough if it produced no obstacles.

Look back over the goals you wrote for each of the seven major areas of your life. What roadblocks would keep you from achieving those goals? Suppose you have a goal to exercise twenty minutes a day, beginning today. But then you remember you don't have the right shoes to wear. That is a roadblock. That is an obstacle that is relatively easy to overcome. On your "To Do" list for today, you write, "Buy new shoes."

Or, suppose that you have a goal in your spiritual life to share the Gospel with one new person every week. That is certainly a worthy goal. But you realize you don't know how to make a Gospel presentation. That is your roadblock. So your next step of action is to enroll in an evangelism training class at your church, or to go to the local Christian bookstore to find some books or tracts that will aid you in sharing your faith.

But some obstacles are not so easily overcome. Some of us have social, educational, economic, or physical handicaps that are not easily removed. In those cases, perseverance does not mean *removing* the obstacle; it means continuing *in spite of* the obstacle. The Apostle Paul is a perfect illustration of this truth. Paul had numerous handicaps that could have discouraged him from pursuing his purpose in life: to be God's messenger to the Gentiles. First, he was a Jew, (he, of course, had no control over his heritage). Secondly, he was ugly. One account in an apocryphal book *Acts of Paul and Thelca* says, "And he saw Paul coming, a man little of stature, thin-haired upon the head, crooked in the legs, of good state of body, with eyebrows joining, and nose somewhat hooked." Not exactly the kind of guy who would make a successful television evangelist! Third, Paul was not a good communicator. Paul mentioned some of the accusations against himself: "For they say, 'His letters are weighty and strong, but his personal presence is unimpressive, and his speech contemptible' " (2 Cor. 10:10).

But all of these handicaps pale in comparison to his

major handicap—his unspecified "thorn in the flesh." We
do not know for sure what this obstacle was. Most com-
mentators agree that it must have been some type of physical infirmity. Whatever it was, it hindered Paul's preaching
ministry. Thus it is not surprising that Paul asked God to
remove the obstacle. That was a reasonable request. God
was the One who called Paul to be a preacher. Surely He
did not want anything to stand in the way of Paul's achieving his life purpose. Yet God refused to remove the
obstacle:

> Concerning this [thorn in the flesh] I entreated the
> Lord three times that it might depart from me. And He
> said to me, "My grace is sufficient for you, for power
> is perfected in weakness." Most gladly, therefore, I
> will rather boast about my weakness, that the power
> of Christ may dwell in me (2 Cor. 12:8-9).

When Paul ran into a brick wall, he did not quit. Instead,
he began to look at his obstacle from God's point of view.
Paul saw his immovable roadblock as a motivation to trust
God rather than to depend on his own abilities.

All of us will face some unchangeable life circumstances
that will appear to hinder our achieving our goals. We have
two choices in how to respond to such obstacles. We can
give up. Or, we can choose to view those problems as
brilliantly disguised opportunities to trust God.

3. *Realize that failure is not final.* We live in a culture
that teaches, "If at first you don't succeed, give up." And
yet, those who ultimately succeed in achieving their life
purpose are those who refuse to be paralyzed by failure. In
fact, failure is a prerequisite for success.

Thomas J. Watson, the founder of IBM, said, "The way
to succeed is to double your failure rate."[6] In other words,
the more times you try, the more times you will succeed.
Thomas Edison, one of our nation's greatest inventors, discovered at least 1,800 ways *not* to build a light bulb. Babe
Ruth struck out 1,330 times, yet he was considered one of
the greatest baseball players of all time. George Bernard
Shaw had his first five novels rejected. Columbus thought

he was finding a shortcut to India when he discovered America.

No one ever stubbed his toe standing still! The fact is that we do not always know which of our efforts will ultimately bring success. That is why we must always keep trying. Solomon likely had that truth in mind when he wrote, "Cast your bread on the surface of the waters, for you will find it after many days" (Ecc.11:1). Some interpret that verse only in the context of giving money to the poor. But a better understanding of the verse comes from translating "cast" as "send." Solomon was referring to sending ships to foreign countries. Eventually, some of the ships that were dispatched would return with gain. By the way, that is where we get the expression "waiting for your ship to come in."

Motivational speaker Charlie "Tremendous" Jones claims, "A lot of people are waiting for their ship to come in, even though they never sent one out!" Or they only sent out one ship. The more ships you send out—the more times you try—the greater your chances for success.

Several years ago, I was visiting with Virginia Muir, who had served as the secretary and executive assistant to Ken Taylor, the compiler of *The Living Bible* and founder of Tyndale House Publishers. She related to me the exciting story of how Dr. Taylor succeeded in his vision of creating an easily understood paraphrase of the Bible. Dr. Taylor was a businessman in Chicago who spent his commuting time on the train paraphrasing portions of the Bible to use with his children during their evening devotions. His children were so enthusiastic about being able to understand the Bible that Dr. Taylor continued in his project until he had completed the entire New Testament. He thought that others might profit from his work as well, so he submitted it to a Christian publisher. But the publisher rejected Taylor's proposal. Taylor tried a second publisher and was rejected. Eventually, a half dozen publishers said "no" to his proposal. But Ken Taylor did not allow failure to stop him. He and his wife took their life savings and published *The Living Letters* themselves. At first, it was not successful. But today, *The Living Bible* has sold tens of millions of copies and has been translated into dozens of other languages. Furthermore, *The Living Bible* became the foundation for one of the greatest Christian publishing companies in the world. All because Ken Taylor refused to be paralyzed by temporary failure.

4. *Expect to work hard.* Inherent in the exercise of perseverance is what Tim Hansel calls "holy sweat" in his book by the same name. Work without fatigue equals mediocrity. Hard work is a prerequisite for success in every area of life, including our spiritual lives. No, we are not saved *by* works, but we are saved *for* good works: "For by grace you have been saved through faith; and that not of yourselves, it is the gift of God; not as a result of works, that no one should boast. For we are His workmanship, created in Christ Jesus for good works" (Eph. 2:8-10).

Paul writes about the great energy that he exerted in order to be successful in his Christian life: "Therefore I run in such a way, as not without aim; I box in such a way, as not beating the air; but I buffet my body and make it my slave, lest possibly after I have preached to others I myself should be disqualified" (1 Cor. 9:26-27).

We do not want to hear about the necessity for hard work—especially in the Christian life. So, we develop a theology (totally apart from Scripture) that says *no* effort is required to live the Christian life. The truth is that hard work is a non-negotiable essential for success in every area of life. Such a message is not popular in our culture today. We want an immediate pay-off for our efforts, or we will move on to dabble in some other pursuit. Edwin Bliss describes this tendency in his book *Doing It Now:*

> We live in a culture that worships comfort. During this century we have seen the greatest assault on discomfort in the history of the human race. We have learned to control our environment with central heating and air conditioning. We have reduced drudgery with machines and computers. And we have learned to control pain, depression, and stress. We even provide electronic antidotes to the boredom with television sets and video games. Most of this is to the good,

but unfortunately it has created an impression that the purpose of life is to attain a blissful state of nirvana, a total absence of struggle or strain. The emphasis is on consuming not producing; on short-term hedonism rather than long-term satisfaction. We seek immediate gratification of our desires, with no penalties.[7]

But success requires effort and sacrifice. No pain, no gain. And that realization is the essence of perseverance. Dennis Waitley said it best when he said, "The ninth best-kept secret of total success is that winners work at doing things the majority of the population are not willing to do."[8]

Do you desire to achieve the purpose, objectives, and goals God has led you to establish for your life? If so, don't look for immediate fulfillment of those dreams. And don't become discouraged when others seem to be making progress and you seem to be standing still. The words of Amy Carmichael have often encouraged me:

Sometimes when we read the words of those
who have been more
than conquerors, we feel almost despondent.
I feel that I shall never be like that.
But they won through step-by-step
by little bits of wills,
little denials of self,
little inward victories,
by faithfulness in very little things.
They became what they are. No one sees these little
hidden steps. They only see the accomplishment, but
even so, those small steps were taken.
There is no sudden triumph
no spiritual maturity.
That is the work of the moment.[9]

Perseverance—refusing to give up despite the inevitable roadblocks that life erects—is an attitude that will insure the realization of your God-given goals.

CHAPTER FOUR

CHOOSING FAITH OVER WORRY

"For God has not given us a spirit of timidity, but of power and love and discipline."   *2 Tim. 1:7*

■ A thief is running loose in our midst — a dangerous thief, robbing us of what is most important in life: joy, energy, peace of mind, and even our health. The name of the thief? Worry.

Though there may not be much basis for our worry, it nevertheless can cause us to lose all sense of perspective. Someone has said that worry is "a thin stream of fear trickling through the mind. If encouraged, it cuts a channel into which all other thoughts are drained." The word *worry* comes from a German word which means "to strangle." Worry literally strangles us spiritually, emotionally, and even physically. Author Corrie Ten Boom once said, "Worry doesn't empty tomorrow of its sorrow; it empties today of its strength."

The devastating power of worry was demonstrated during World War II. From 1941-45, 250,000 Americans were killed in combat. During that period, 2 million Americans died of cardiovascular disease. Physicians said that one-third to one-half of those deaths were related to worry. Amazing! More Americans were killed by anxiety than by war. Dr. Charles Mayo, founder of the internationally known Mayo Clinic, was probably correct when he said that half of our hospital beds are filled with people who worried themselves there.[1]

Worry not only drains us emotionally and physically, but it can also sap our spiritual strength. In Luke 8, Jesus told a parable about a sower who went out to sow his seed. The seed fell on different types of soil. Most of the seed did not grow because it fell on the wrong type of soil. The seed, Jesus said, represents the Word of God. The soils are symbolic of the different conditions of the human heart. Notice one type of soil in which the seed did not grow: "And the seed which fell among the thorns, these are the ones who have heard, and as they go on their way they are choked with worries and riches and pleasures of this life, and bring no fruit to maturity" (Luke 8:14).

Of all the things that are responsible for hindering a person's spiritual growth, notice what heads the list. Worry! Although the world is plagued with anxiety, God never intended His children to be overtaken by it. In fact, Jesus Christ left us with a potent antidote to worry: "Peace I leave with you; My peace I give to you; not as the world gives, do I give to you. Let not your heart be troubled, nor let it be fearful" (John 14:27).

We appropriate Christ's gift of peace through the attitude of faith. Faith is not a hope or a wish, but it is a confidence that God is going to take care of us. The writer of Hebrews defined faith this way: "Now faith is the assurance of things hoped for, the conviction of things not seen (11:1). Faith is not just a positive emotion we try to create when life unravels. Instead, it is the assurance that no matter what happens, God is still in control.

Most of us have to admit that we are not enjoying the gift of peace that Christ left us. Why? Because we *choose* worry over peace. Anxiety is an attitude choice. Remember the definition of an attitude? An attitude is "our mental and emotional response to the circumstances of life." The moment we are faced with a negative circumstance, we can respond in one of two ways. We can choose to worry about the situation, or we can choose to believe that God is in control of this circumstance and will take care of us. Before we look at some ways to develop the attitude of faith, let's first examine some of the causes of worry.

■ *Causes of Worry*

Think for just a moment about what you fear most in life. Then, write down your three greatest fears:

Fear #1:

Fear #2:

Fear #3:

I imagine that most of your fears involve something being taken away from you—a person, a position, or a possession. Maybe you are afraid that you will lose your spouse, either through death or desertion. Possibly, you are worried about losing your job and, as a result, your prestige. Or, maybe you are fearful of losing your money and facing poverty. The loss of your health might also be a potent source of anxiety.

Most worry involves the fear of losing something important to us. Thus a major cause of worry is building our lives around temporal things. The Great Scottish preacher Alexander Whyte once wrote about our tendency to "hang very heavy weights on very thin wires." For example, we hang the heavy weight of our happiness on the very thin wire of health, only to have it snapped by a negative report from the doctor. Or we hang the heavy weight of our security on the thin wire of our job, only to have the wire snapped by a change in the economy. Or we hang the heavy weight of purpose in life on our family, only to have it snapped by a traffic fatality. We will always be anxious whenever we build our lives around anyone or anything that can be taken away from us.

Most of us think the way to remove anxiety is to protect ourselves from adversity. For example, if we are fearful about poverty, we will accumulate all the money we can and place it in a safe investment. If we are anxious about our health, we will diet, exercise, and see a doctor about any anomaly. If we are anxious about losing the affection of someone important to us, we will smother that person with attention. Unfortunately, it is impossible to prevent every possible loss.

The following true account illustrates the futility of trying to remove anxiety through self-effort. J.H. Zorthian, a famous mural artist, read about a young boy who had been killed in a traffic accident. He became extremely anxious as he contemplated the possibility of losing one of his children in such a tragedy. He became so obsessed by this fear that he was unable to work.

At last he surrendered to his obsession. Canceling his negotiations to purchase a large house in busy Pasadena, he began to seek a place where his children would be safe. His pursuit became so intense he set aside all his work while scheming and planning every possible means to protect his children from harm. He tried to imagine the presence of danger in everything. . . . He bought twelve acres perched on a mountain at the end of a long, winding, narrow road. At each turn along the road he posted signs, "Children at Play." Before starting construction on the house itself, Zorthian personally built and fenced a play yard for his three children. He built it in such a way that it was impossible for a car to get within fifty feet of it. . . . Finally, the garage was to be built. Only one automobile ever drove into that garage—Zorthian's.

He stood back and surveyed every possibility of danger to his children. He could think of only one remaining hazard. He had to back in and out of the garage—he might, in some hurried moment, back over one of the children. He immediately made plans for a protected turnaround. The contractor returned and set the forms for that additional area, but before the cement could be poured, a downpour stopped the project. . . .

If it had not rained that week the concrete turnaround

would have been completed and been in use by Sunday. That was February 9, 1947. . . . the day his eighteen-month-old son, Tiran, squirmed away from his sister's grasp and ran behind the car as Zorthian drove it from the garage. The child was killed instantly.[2]

Jesus reminds us that loss of relationships or possessions is inevitable: "Do not lay up for yourselves treasures upon earth, where moth and rust destroy, and where thieves break in and steal. But lay up for yourselves treasures in heaven, where neither moth nor rust destroys, and where thieves do not break in or steal" (Matt. 6:19-20). That is why it is much wiser to build our happiness around those things that can not be taken away from us.

D.L. Moody once said, "Trust in yourself and you are doomed to disappointment; trust in your friends and they will die and leave you; trust in money and it may be taken from you; trust in reputation and some slanderous tongue may blast it; but trust in God, and you are never to be confounded in time or eternity."

■ Anxiety Caused by Sin

Some of our anxiety in life results from sinful behavior. Whenever we consciously and willfully violate God's standards, we sense that judgment is coming. We fear that God is going to get even with us. Sometimes we fear that our sinful behavior is going to be uncovered. Undoubtedly, that was David's problem after he committed adultery with Bathsheba and murdered her husband, Uriah. For months, David lived in constant dread that his sin would be discovered: "When I kept silent about my sin, my body wasted away through my groaning all day long. For day and night Thy hand was heavy upon me; my vitality was drained away as with the fever heat of summer" (Ps. 32:3-4).

Other times, our disobedient lifestyles produce a general sense of uneasiness. We don't know for sure what form our judgment will take, but we know it is certain. The proverbial Sword of Damacles hangs over our heads, ready to drop at any time. Such general fear is what seventeenth century theologian Jonathan Edwards had in mind when he said,

"The unrighteous tremble at the rustling of the leaves."

Conversely, righteous living produces peace of mind. The Prophet Isaiah wrote, "And the work of righteousness will be peace, and the service of righteousness, quietness and confidence forever" (32:17).

Such peace of mind is beautifully illustrated in Daniel's life. God's young servant was the target of a devious plot by the King's commissioners. Jealous over Daniel's rise to power, they encouraged Darius to sign an edict prohibiting prayer to any sovereign other than Darius. The punishment for breaking the injunction was death.

But such a law could not deter Daniel from serving God. Notice Daniel's calm response, when he heard that the edict had been signed: "Now when Daniel knew that the document was signed, he entered his house (now in his roof chamber he had windows open toward Jerusalem); and he continued kneeling on his knees three times a day, praying and giving thanks before his God, as he had been doing previously" (Dan. 6:10).

Contrast Daniel's serenity to Darius' anxiety: "Then the king went off to his palace and spent the night fasting, and no entertainment was brought before him; and his sleep fled from him" (6:18). Daniel was free from worry because he was obedient to God. On the other hand, Darius knew that even though his edict was consistent with the law of the Medes and Persians, he was violating God's standards. And such an awareness produced fear.

■ *Worry: Satan's Flaming Missile*

Satanic attacks are a third source of anxiety. Paul discusses the armor available for use against Satanic attack in Ephesians 6:13-18. Look at verse 16: "In addition to all, taking up the shield of faith with which you will be able to extinguish all the flaming missiles of the evil one."

In Paul's day, the Roman shield was a piece of wood, two and one-half feet wide, and four and one-half feet high, that was covered with metal or leather soaked in water. The enemy would often shoot an arrow that had been soaked in pitch and ignited. Because the flaming arrow would ignite anything it hit, the only protection available against serious burns was this shield, soaked in water. When the flaming missile hit the shield, it was immediately extinguished.

Satan has a large arsenal of flaming missiles at his disposal. One missile is lust; another, doubt; another, depression. But one of his favorite arrows, I believe, is labeled "anxiety." Why?

First, look at the result of anxiety. When this missile strikes us, we are paralyzed by it. Fear is like a stun gun that leaves us incapable of performing our God-given responsibilities. Worry is so overwhelming that we are usually incapable of doing anything else. Does such an emotion come from God? Sometimes. We have seen that building our lives around temporal values or living a disobedient life can produce anxiety. And God uses such anxiety to bring us into a right relationship with Himself.

But many times, anxiety is the direct result of Satanic attack—especially when such fear hinders our relationship with God instead of encouraging it. Have you ever been so anxious that the last thing you felt like doing was praying, reading God's Word, or confronting your fear in a rational way? Such paralyzing fear does not come from God. "For God has not given us the spirit of timidity, but of power and love and discipline" (2 Tim. 1:7).

Another reason I believe that most anxiety is a result of Satanic attack is that worry usually is not built on fact but on lies. Jesus said that Satan is the father of lies (John 8:44). Dr. Walter Cavert, in his study of anxiety, concluded that only 8 percent of peoples' worries were legitimate. In other words, 92 percent of our worries are without foundation![3] Such unfounded worry is a favorite weapon of the Evil One.

Not long ago while working in my church office, I was hit by an anxiety arrow, causing me to suddenly be overwhelmed by the thought that I was going to die soon of some dreaded disease. I will admit that there was some basis for the fear—both my parents died from cancer at a relatively young age. But I had no objective reason to believe that I was ill. Nevertheless, I was so overcome with worry that I could not continue my work. Instead, I began calling doctor friends I knew, describing my fear, my aches and pains, and my family history! Everyone was reassuring, except my insurance agent who highly recommended I consider some additional life insurance coverage. I wasted several hours of valuable time that afternoon because I did not raise my shield of faith.

■ *Choosing Faith over Anxiety*

How do we erect the shield of faith to extinguish Satan's anxiety arrows? Let me suggest four positive actions to alleviate anxiety.

1. Repent of known sin in your life. If the major sources of anxiety are building one's life around temporal values or living in disobedience to God's commands, then it seems logical that the way to remove anxiety would be to turn from those attitudes or actions. And that is what the word *repent* means, to turn around.

To constantly fear losing something or someone close to you is the result of an improper value system. Such anxiety reveals that your affections are not centered around the Creator but around His creation. And such misplaced love is idolatry. When we think of idolatry, we conjure up images of heathens bowing down before a small wooden image or dancing naked around a golden calf. We would never be guilty of that!

But when we love anyone or anything more than God, we are committing idolatry. And we are also setting the stage for a life of worry. Why? Because anything less than God can be taken from us. And deep down we know that. So our lives are spent frantically trying to hold on to that which we know can be taken from us in a moment. What is the cure for such misplaced affection? "If then you have been raised up with Christ, keep seeking the things above, where Christ is, seated at the right hand of God. Set your mind on the things above, not on the things that are on earth" (Col. 3:1-2).

In addition to changing attitudes, you may need to change some of your actions to reduce anxiety. As mentioned, a Christian engaging in sinful behavior instinctively knows that judgment is coming. I remember a particularly painful period in my life when I was living apart from God. I was engaging in activities that were completely contrary to God's standards. What I remember most about that time was the tremendous anxiety that I constantly felt. I was convinced that God was going to chastise me. So I "trembled at the rustling of the leaves," as Edwards said. Every problem at work, every ache and pain I felt, every financial setback, was viewed as a precursor to "the coming judgment."

Such fear is not without basis. God does discipline His children: "For those whom the Lord loves He disciplines, and He scourges every son whom He receives" (Heb. 12:6). Had I continued in my sin, I no doubt would have felt the judgment of God in my life.

But a Christian does not have to live in fear of God's discipline. He can remove the fear of impending doom by simply turning away from his sin. Paul said it succinctly: "But if we judged ourselves rightly, we should not be judged" (1 Cor. 11:31).

2. Remove unnecessary fear. Much of the anxiety we suffer is unnecessary and can be easily removed. How? By confronting the source of our fears. Many of us feel anxious about things we know we should be doing but are not doing. For example, you know you should go to the dentist to have your teeth cleaned, but you are afraid of what a checkup might reveal. So you keep postponing the appointment. Unfortunately, you cannot postpone your anxiety. You know that your teeth are suffering from neglect. So you continue to be infected with a low-grade case of anxiety. You don't think about your teeth every day. But on the backburner of your mind, you have just added one more source of worry.

Or maybe you have not reconciled your bank statement in several months. You are afraid that you will find that you have less money than you thought. So you put it off until next month. But every time you write a check, you wonder if this is going to be the one that bounces.

A doctor has said that the three killers of our age are the telephone, the clock, and the calendar. What do these three items have in common? They all remind us of what we should be doing. And such reminders produce anxiety. Here are three words that will help you remove much of the anxiety in your life: *do it now!*

If there is a telephone call to be made, *do it now!*
If there is a difficult letter to be written, *do it now!*
If there is an appointment to be made, *do it now!*

Another way to confront unnecessary anxiety is to learn to deal realistically with your anxiety. Remember that Satan attacks us with unfounded fear. But such fear is easily dissipated when confronted with truth. Willard Scott, NBC's teddy bear weatherman on "The Today Show," tells of being deathly afraid of bridges. He would avoid them at every opportunity. Tired of the inconvenience of avoiding bridges, he decided to face his fear head-on. He got in his convertible and crossed the bridge over Chesapeake Bay forty times! And guess what? The bridge did not collapse. Scott had confronted his fear with truth.

Some years ago, I was returning from a mission trip to Mexico. While sitting in the Mexico City airport, I was overwhelmed by fear. After doing a quick spiritual life check-up, I realized that my anxiety was not the result of any known sin in my life. Sensing that this fear was one of Satan's anxiety darts, I decided to confront my fear. I pulled out a yellow legal pad and wrote across the top of the page the particular fear I was experiencing. Then, I divided the page into three columns. The first column was titled, "Reasons This Probably Will Not Happen." I listed five good reasons that this fear was totally unfounded. The second column was titled "What I Would Do if This Did Happen." I then listed my steps of action in the event that this fear came true. I found that this exercise made me realize that I could survive such a mishap. Finally, the third column was headed "Benefits of This Event." I thought of five positive benefits of my fear coming true.

The result of this activity was that my fear soon departed. I have kept that piece of paper in my files as a reminder that one good way to alleviate anxiety is to confront it. And such action is biblical. Another piece of the

Christian's armor mentioned in Ephesians is the belt of truth: "Stand firm therefore, having girded your loins with truth" (Eph. 6:14). The loose ends of a soldier's tunic were tucked into his belt, so that he would not trip. In the same way, we are to gird or tuck in our loose thoughts into the belt of truth. That is what Peter had in mind when he wrote, "Therefore, gird your minds for action" (1 Peter 1:13). Tuck any loose thoughts into the belt of truth so that you might not stumble.

3. Remember God's past faithfulness. As you read the Psalms, you quickly realize that David suffered from anxiety attacks. One of his particularly acute attacks is recorded in Psalm 3. As his son Absalom led a national revolt against his father, David lapsed into despair: "O Lord, how my adversaries have increased! Many are rising up against me. Many are saying of my soul, 'There is no deliverance for him in God' " (Ps. 3:1-2).

But then notice how quickly David's attitude changes: "But Thou, O Lord, art a shield about me, my glory, and the One who lifts my head. I was crying to the Lord with my voice, and He answered me from His holy mountain. I lay down and slept; I awoke, for the Lord sustains me. I will not be afraid of ten thousands of people who have set themselves against me round about" (Ps. 3:3-6).

What accounts for David's new courage? I believe that David started to remember God's past faithfulness to Him. And such reflection reminded David that God was completely capable and willing to sustain him now. David had a habit of remembering God's faithfulness. When he was confronted by the giant Goliath, he remarked, "The Lord who delivered me from the paw of the lion and from the paw of the bear, He will deliver me from the hand of this Philistine" (1 Sam. 17:37). Now, as David faced an equally formidable enemy, he was able to add to his list of memories of God's prior faithfulness. "As God delivered me from the paw of the lion and bear, as he delivered me from Goliath, as he delivered me from Saul, he will certainly deliver me from Absalom."

In the same way, I believe that God wants us to have a pool of memories to draw from in times of adversity. Such memories of God's prior faithfulness can relieve anxiety. Specifically, I would suggest that you keep a journal of your prayer requests, making sure to date each request and record the answer to that request. My prayer diary is a great source of comfort as I am able to look back and see God's past faithfulness to me.

4. Remain in contact with God. The two greatest antidotes to anxiety are found in Philippians 4:6-9. One involves our communication with God; the other antidote is allowing God to communicate to us.

First, notice the relationship between prayer and worry: "Be anxious for nothing, but in everything by prayer and supplication with thanksgiving let your requests be made known to God. And the peace of God, which surpasses all comprehension, shall guard your hearts and your minds in Christ Jesus (Phil. 4:6-7).

Talking to God about your fears causes His peace to "guard your hearts and your minds." Paul was alluding here to a Roman guard that marched around a fortress. God's peace marches around our hearts and minds when we talk to Him.

The second cure for worry is allowing God to speak to us through His Word: "Finally, brethren, whatever is true, whatever is honorable, whatever is right, whatever is pure, whatever is lovely, whatever is of good repute, if there is any excellence, and if anything worthy of praise, let your mind dwell on these things. . . . And the God of peace shall be with you" (4:8-9).

I believe that when Paul speaks of dwelling on whatever is true, honorable, pure, and lovely, he is referring to the Word of God. Psalm 19:7-10 uses many of those phrases to describe God's Word. The Bible is a record of both God's past faithfulness and God's future promises to His children. And such a record is an eternal source of relief from worry.

Prayer and meditation on God's Word freed Paul from many anxious moments in that Roman prison. And such peace of mind is available to anyone who will choose faith in God over anxiety.

CHAPTER FIVE

CHOOSING REPENTANCE OVER GUILT

"As I live, says the Lord God, I have no pleasure in the death of the wicked; I desire that the wicked turn from his evil ways and live. Turn, turn from your wickedness, for why will you die?... The sins of an evil man will not destroy him if he repents and turns from his sins."

Ezek. 33:11-12, TLB

■ The following note in the thief's handwriting was found in a stolen Trans Am returned by police to its owner in Los Angeles:

Your CB is in the trunk box. The radio is out because I couldn't stop my friend from taking it (insurance will cover radio). I'm sorry it had to be your car, but I was looking for one and the car lot left the key in and unattended. Your left back tire loses a little air at times. Your brake light comes on a lot and sometimes stays on when you drive (check your brakes). I hope this didn't put you out for me taking your car. I would have preferred a dealer's car. But this was all that was available. Sorry (needs gas).[1]

Everyone—including car thieves—at one time or another faces moral failure. How do we deal with such failure? We have a choice. We can choose to ignore it or we can repent. Repentance is an attitude that chooses to confront failure rather than ignore it. And such an attitude choice is absolutely vital to our physical, emotional, and spiritual health.

Unfortunately, most of us have a limited view of repentance. We tend to think of repentance only in terms of salvation. The word *repent* conjures up images of some straggly street preacher announcing the end of the world via a sandwich board. Yet, an examination of Scripture reveals that repentance is an attitude that is more characteristic of Christians than of non-Christians. It is not just a one-time action that insures heaven after we die. Instead, repentance is an attitude that confronts and deals with failure in every area of life. Martin Luther understood this truth. The first of the Ninety-five Theses he nailed to the church door at Wittenberg read, "When our Lord and Master Jesus Christ said 'repent,' He willed that the entire life of believers be one of repentance."

■ *Definition of Repentance*

Contrary to popular opinion, repentance is not an emotion; but it is an attitude that leads to a specific action. The Greek verb *metanoeo*, which is translated "repent," means "to change one's mind." The word pictures someone headed in one direction who, because of a change of mind, starts going in another direction. Maybe you have had the experience of driving down a street and suddenly noticing that all of the street signs are backwards and every other car is headed in the opposite direction (including those in your lane!) What do you do? You make a quick U-turn and head in the opposite direction in order to avoid some serious consequences. In the same way, repentance both honestly acknowledges failure and causes a change of direction.

Repentance is not a popular topic today, because it requires us to honestly confront sin. None of us likes to be reminded of our faults. As the writer Maurice Samuel put it, "No man loves his alarm clock." And yet the failure to confront sin can have a much more severe consequence than driving the wrong way down a one-way street or refusing to set an alarm clock. What is the result of not repenting? In a word, guilt.

■ *The Problem with Guilt*

Guilt is one of the most debilitating of human emotions. It wreaks destruction in our relationships and in our spiritual lives. It is also a major cause of depression. The disastrous effects of guilt are demonstrated in the life of King David, as mentioned in chapter 4. David was the most successful of all of Israel's kings. He led the nation to new heights of prosperity and power. And he was a man after God's own heart. But he traded all of those things for one night of passion involving Bathsheba (2 Sam. 11:2-5). In an instant he made a wrong choice that led to the sins of adultery and murder.

How did David deal with this embarrassing situation related to Bathsheba becoming pregnant? By a royal cover-up that surpassed Watergate! David decided to call Bathsheba's husband, Uriah, in from the front lines, thinking he would surely sleep with his wife. Then everyone would think Uriah was the father of the baby. Although the plan sounded reasonable to David, it did not work out as David had planned. Uriah chose not to sleep with his wife.

At this point David could have chosen to confront his sin. But instead, he engaged in an even more elaborate plan to cover his tracks. This time he ordered that Uriah be placed in the front lines of battle to be killed. Then after Uriah's death, David took Bathsheba as his wife. It was, of course, nothing less than murder, and "the thing that David had done was evil in the sight of the Lord" (2 Sam. 11:14-15, 26-27).

Days and even months went by without any visible judgment from God. Why was God delaying His punishment? David made the same mistake that we make in our concept of God's justice. We think that God is overlooking our sins just because He does not discipline us immediately. We confuse God's mercy with God's tolerance of sin. Yet God sometimes delays judgment so that we might repent. The writer of Ecclesiastes understood this truth when he wrote, "Because the sentence against an evil deed is not executed quickly, therefore the hearts of the sons of men among them are given fully to do evil" (8:11).

Although there were no external signs of God's judgment during the months after David's sins, God was still dealing with the king internally. David was living under a load of guilt that was draining him physically, emotionally, and spiritually, as noted when we discussed the problem of anxiety. "When I kept silent about my sin, my body wasted away through my groaning all day long. For day and night Thy hand was heavy upon me; My vitality was drained away as with the fever heat of summer" (Ps. 32:3-4).

First, notice the physical effects of guilt: "my body wasted away . . . my vitality was drained." A connection between guilt and physical illness is recognized today by psychologists and psychiatrists. In his book *Head First: The Biology of Hope*, Norman Cousins explains, "They [psychologists and psychiatrists] recognize that awareness of wrongdoing often produces prolonged feelings of remorse and self-condemnation that, lacking catharsis, can actually have damaging effects on the bodily systems and open the gates to disease."[2]

I remember reading about one of the engineers involved in the fatal *Challenger* launch. Although he tried to stop the launch, the engineer still had feelings of guilt long after the tragedy. "I have headaches. I cry. I have bad dreams. I go into a hypnotic trance almost daily." The physical effects of unresolved guilt can range from simple sluggishness to a breakdown in the immune system that leads to serious disease.

Guilt also affects us emotionally. The most common emotional manifestation of guilt is depression. David uses the phrase "groaning all day long" to describe his depression. What is the connection between guilt and depression? Most psychiatrists agree that there are times our guilt and resulting depression are not justified. Psychiatrists refer to these unjustified feelings as false guilt. The obsessive-compulsive personality (perfectionist) is most likely to experience false guilt. A salesman who fails to meet his self-imposed quota for the month, or a housewife who is unable to continually make her home look like the cover of *Better Homes and Gardens* magazine may experience false guilt.

Such guilt comes from setting unrealistic standards for oneself. And some of those unrealistic standards can even be spiritual. The engaged couple who believe that a kiss before marriage is a no-no are probably good candidates for a load of false guilt. Such standards are unrealistic and have no foundation in God's Word.

Psychiatrists talk about false guilt. Some, like Freud, think all guilt is false guilt. Such a belief stems from failing to believe that there are absolute standards of behavior. As Christians, we realize that we are obligated to act in a certain manner. When we fail to do so, we feel guilty bcause we are guilty. Most guilt, therefore, is true guilt. Christian psychiatrists Frank Minirth and Paul Meier write, "In our experience as psychiatrists, when people have told us they feel guilty, it has usually been true guilt. They feel guilty because they *are* guilty. And straightening out the wrong they are doing is sometimes all that is needed to straighten out their feelings of depression."[3]

It is important to note that depression and repentance are not synonymous terms. One can be upset with himself over his failure, or the results of his failure, without ever actually repenting.

As I write these words, I have just finished counseling a man who has been involved in an illicit relationship for a number of years. The girl in the relationship has discovered she is pregnant and has married another man. The father of the baby explained to me that he carries a disease which threatens both the life of the mother and the baby. He is deeply depressed over losing his lover and at the prospect of her and his child dying as the result of his actions. Yet there is no hint that he plans to change anything in his life as a result of this episode. He is remorseful but not repentant.

The Apostle Paul contrasted sorrow (depression) with

repentance in 2 Corinthians 7:10: "For the sorrow that is according to the will of God produces a repentance without regret, leading to salvation; but the sorrow of the world produces death." More will be said about the difference between remorse and repentance when we discuss how to develop an attitude of repentance.

Another emotional effect of guilt is anxiety. I imagine that David lived in constant fear that at some point his secret would be revealed. The fact that he engaged in such an elaborate scheme to cover up his actions proves how much he dreaded being discovered. And, of course, his worst nightmare became a reality. One day, Nathan the prophet came to visit David. The prophet told a story about a rich man who took a poor man's only possession, a little ewe lamb. David, enraged over this injustice, demanded to know the identity of the scoundrel. Without missing a beat, Nathan replied, "You are the man. . . . Thus says the Lord, 'Behold, I will raise up evil against you from your own household. . . . Indeed you did it secretly, but I will do this thing before all Israel, and under the sun" (2 Sam. 12:7, 11-12). A common by-product of guilt is the unrelenting fear that judgment is about to be administered. And certainly such a feeling is usually justified.

Guilt not only impairs us physically and emotionally, but it has serious ramifications in our spiritual lives. David said, "For day and night Thy hand was heavy upon me" (Ps. 32:4). There are several spiritual consequences of unresolved guilt. One is a break in our fellowship with God. James alludes to this when he describes the cycle of sin: "Then when lust has conceived, it gives birth to sin; and when sin is accomplished, it brings forth death" (James 1:15). The end result of unresolved guilt is death.

What does James mean by "death"? Physical death? Possibly. The Bible certainly teaches that Christians who continue in sin are subject to premature death (see 1 Corinthians 11:28-30). And yet, such judgment seems to be more the exception than the rule. Is James speaking of spiritual death? Probably not, since he addresses believers, who have been delivered from the eternal consequences of sin.

What does James mean by sin resulting in death? The Greek word for death is *thanatos.* It literally means "separation." Physical death is the separation of the spirit from the body. Spiritual death is the eternal separation of our spirit from God. Since James is addressing Christians, I believe he is referring to a deathlike existence in the life of a Christian who fails to repent. Such a Christian is living apart from God, just as David did for the months he refused to confess his sins. During that period of time, David did not enjoy the benefits of his relationship with God. Instead, he felt the heavy hand of God upon his life. David no longer saw God as a friend but as a foe.

It is important to understand that David's position in God's eyes never changed. Sin never changes God's attitude toward true believers. But sin changes *our* attitudes about God. Guilt breaks a relationship between two people—even when only one of the parties feels guilty. For example, have you ever borrowed money from someone and then felt uncomfortable around that person? Though the other party may not be concerned about it, you feel awkward about it and do your best to avoid the person.

It is the same in our relationship with God. Guilt causes us to want to avoid God. Why? Because guilt causes our perception of God to change from that of a loving Father to a vindictive deity waiting to punish us. Remember the story of Adam and Eve? After violating God's one prohibition, their response was to run and hide:

> And they heard the sound of the Lord God walking in the garden in the cool of the day, and the man and his wife hid themselves from the presence of the Lord God among the trees of the garden. Then the Lord God called to the man, and said to him, "Where are you?" And he said, "I heard the sound of Thee in the garden, and I was afraid because I was naked; so I hid myself (Gen. 3:8-10).

One spiritual effect of guilt is a broken relationship with God—not because God has changed His attitude about us, but because we have changed our attitude about Him.

But there is another spiritual consequence of unresolved guilt. When David wrote about experiencing God's heavy hand, I do not think he was only referring to the emotional turmoil in his life. I believe David was also experiencing the discipline of God. We do not know what form God's discipline may have taken during this period of unresolved guilt—it may have been chaos in David's home or in the kingdom. But one fact is certain, God chastises His children who continue in sin. The purpose of such discipline is never retribution but restoration.

When our daughter, Julia, was two years old, she climbed onto the kitchen table at times. After explaining to her that she could fall and hurt herself, we resorted to spanking her when she began to climb up on the table. Why? Not out of anger, but for her own well-being.

In a similar way, God disciplines His children so they will not continue in a destructive form of behavior. Such discipline is evidence of God's love:

> For those whom the Lord loves He disciplines, and He scourges every son whom He receives. It is for discipline that you endure; God deals with you as with sons; for what son is there whom his father does not discipline? But if you are without discipline, of which all have become partakers, then you are illegitimate children and not sons (Heb. 12:6-8).

One word of caution. The story of Job should remind us that not all calamity is the result of God's discipline. Some suffering is simply the result of living in a fallen world (see Luke 13:1-5). Other hardships can be the result of obedience to God (2 Tim. 3:12). Sometimes, God allows trials so that his power might be demonstrated to others in our weakness (2 Cor. 12:7-10). A Christian must ask for God's guidance in discerning whether or not his suffering is the result of God's discipline.

While the discipline of God is never pleasant to experience, it sometimes results in a desire to repent. Recently, a man was in my office detailing the tremendous turmoil in his life—his wife had left him, his business had collapsed, and his health was deteriorating. When I asked him about his spiritual life, he admitted that he was living far away from God. He did not argue when I suggested that maybe God was allowing these circumstances so that he might restore his relationship with God. "Preacher, I just have one question. Where do I start?" Fortunately, the road to repentance is quite simple.

■ *Developing an Attitude of Repentance*
If you are tired of the physical, emotional, and spiritual consequences of guilt, these five steps of action will help you develop an attitude of repentance:

1. *Identify areas of your life where you have failed to meet God's standards.* The first step in repentance is an honest evaluation of every part of your life. Are there areas where you have failed to meet God's expectations? The psalmist prayed, "Search me, O God, and know my heart; try me and know my anxious thoughts; and see if there be any hurtful way in me, and lead me in the everlasting way" (Ps. 139:23-24). Although this list is not exhaustive, let me suggest some different life areas you might probe in order to identify legitimate failure. Take a moment to write down specific ways you have failed to meet God's standards in these areas:

Your relationship with God (unconfessed sin, unkept promises, failure to spend time with Him):

Your relationship with your family (parents and siblings):

Your relationship with your spouse:

Your relationship with your children:

Your relationship with others (immoral relationships, people you have offended, friendships that need to be Christ-centered):

Your habits:

Your possessions (trusting in money, dishonest dealings, failure to be a good steward):

2. *Acknowledge your failure to God.* Whether your guilt involves other people or not, you must realize that all sin is against God. In Psalm 51, the record of David's confession of his sins, the king makes an interesting statement: "Against Thee, Thee only, I have sinned, and done what is evil in Thy sight" (v. 4). In fact, David not only sinned against God, but he sinned against Bathsheba, Uriah, his own family, and the entire kingdom. But the starting place of David's confession was with God. Repentance begins with humbling yourself before God by acknowledging your failure. Such an acknowledgment does not require the wearing of sack cloth or walking on hot coals. To humble yourself before God means to sincerely acknowledge your failure and your need for forgiveness.

3. *Accept God's forgiveness.* The great truth of the Bible is that when we ask God to forgive us, He always responds affirmatively. 1 John 1:9 declares, "If we confess our sins, he is faithful and righteous to forgive us of our sins and to cleanse us from all unrighteousness." David understood that when God forgave his sin, God also forgot about it: "Purify me with hyssop, and I shall be clean; wash me, and I shall be whiter than snow . . . Hide Thy face from my sins, and blot out all of my iniquities (Ps. 51:7, 9).

Do you know people who say, "I will forgive you, but I will not forget"? What they are really saying is, "I will file this offense away until I need it." Fortunately, God does not deal with us in that manner. The phrases "purify me," "wash me," "hide Thy face," and "blot out" all convey the idea of erasing sin, not just temporarily ignoring it. And that is the very essence of the Gospel. God does not say to us, "I am forgiving your sin, but in case you ever mess up again, remember, I have a list of every sin you have ever committed." Instead, He says there is no longer any record of our offenses.

David expanded on this truth in Psalm 32:1-2. Remember, David was writing about the relief he felt from God's forgiveness, in contrast to the months he suffered from unresolved guilt: "How blessed is he whose transgression is forgiven, whose sin is covered! How blessed is the man to whom the Lord does not impute iniquity, and in whose spirit there is no deceit!"

The phrase "does not impute iniquity" is an allusion to entering a debt into a bookkeeping journal. For the Christian, no record is kept of any debt. As Jesus said in John 19:30, the debt has been "Paid in full."

4. *Make restitution where necessary.* Sometimes the nature of our sins demands that we do more than simply ask for God's forgiveness. If we have wronged another person, it is necessary for us to seek that person's forgiveness. In fact, asking others whom we have offended to forgive us takes precedence over worshiping God. Jesus said, "If therefore you are presenting your offering at the altar, and there remember that your brother has something against you, leave your offering there before the altar, and go your way; first be reconciled to your brother, then come and present your offering" (Matt. 5:23-24).

Monetary restitution might also be in order. Zaccheus, the tax collector who was converted, realized that he needed to do more than simply ask the forgiveness of those he had cheated! Without any prompting from Jesus, he volunteered to pay each person four times the amount of money he had stolen from them! Such an action is a sign of genuine repentance.

5. *Turn away from known sin in your life.* It is possible to follow the first steps without ever truly repenting. Remember, the word *repent* carries the idea of turning around. When David asked for God's forgiveness, he also asked for something else—a steadfast spirit: "Create in me

a clean heart, O God, and renew a steadfast spirit within me" (Ps. 51:10).

In the Hebrew mind, the heart was the location of a person's plans and thoughts. David realized that his previous way of thinking had led him into his present desperate situation. True repentance necessitated a new game plan for his life. Psalm 51:5-6 indicates that David examined his "innermost being" to see if there was any area of his life displeasing to God (see also Psalm 139: 23-24). True repentance meant that David would not only identify those areas but would also plan to change them.

You have already identified some areas of your life that need improvement. Now take a few moments to write out some positive actions to take to correct those failures. (Use a sheet of paper for a more complete listing.)

YOUR FAILURES   HOW TO CORRECT
                       YOUR FAILURES

■ *A New Direction*

In a remote portion of Canada, lies the small village of Wabush. For many years, it was completely isolated. However, a road was recently cut through the wilderness to reach this tiny town. Wabush now has one road leading into it, and thus only one road leading out. If someone would travel the unpaved road for six to eight hours to get into Wabush, there would be only one way to leave—by turning around.

You may have been traveling down the road of unresolved guilt for a long time. Don't be discouraged. There *is* a way out. Decide you are tired of going in that direction; ask for God's forgiveness, make any necessary restitution, and *turn around*.

CHAPTER SIX

CHOOSING RELAXATION OVER STRESS

*"Come to Me, all who are
weary and heavy-laden,
and I will give you rest."*
Matt. 11:28

■ When trying to define obscenity, a Supreme Court justice said, "I may not be able to define it, but I know it when I see it!" The same might be said about attempting to define stress—you may not be able to define it, but you know it when you feel it. In fact, many people are feeling stress today. Ulcers, high blood pressure, migraines, certain strokes, even cancer are just some of the symptoms of a stressed-out society. It is no coincidence that the top selling drugs today are the ulcer medication Tagamet, the tranquilizer Valium, and the cardiac drug Inderal.[1]

And Christians are not exempt from the stress mess. One popular television preacher asked his electronic congregation to name their most pressing problem. Thousands wrote, most listing stress as their number one concern. Unfortunately, preachers and Bible teachers do little to alleviate problems with stress. Instead, we add to the burdens of stressed-out listeners. Consider this quote from author and Bible teacher John MacArthur:

Some of God's most faithful and fruitful saints have lived to old age and been active and productive in His service to the end. Many others, however, have seen their lives shortened for the very reason that they were abounding, overflowing, and untiring, in service to Christ. Henry Martyn, the British missionary to India and Persia, determined to "burn out for God," which he did before he was thirty-five. David Brainerd, one of the earliest missionaries to American Indians, died before he was thirty.[2]

Although the Bible *does* extol the value of hard work for the Christian, this writer seems to be saying, as so many of us preachers and writers do, that "burning out for God" is the highest expression of Christian commitment. I have heard countless Christian workaholics claim, "I would rather burn out than rust out!"

Contrast such a statement with the invitation of Jesus Christ, recorded in Matthew 11:28-30: "Come to Me, all who are weary and heavy-laden, and I will give you rest. Take My yoke upon you, and learn from Me, for I am gentle and humble in heart; and you shall find rest for your souls. For My yoke is easy, and My load is light." Following Jesus Christ should be the cure, not the cause, for a stress-filled life.

Don't misunderstand. Jesus never taught that Christianity is an automatic exemption from problems. In fact, stress is part of the price we pay for living in this world. Consider Christ's words in John 16:33: "These things I have spoken to you, that in Me you may have peace. In the world you have tribulation, but take courage; I have overcome the world." Jesus is not saying that we can live without problems; He says that He offers a way to live *above* problems.

■ *Is Stress Always Harmful?*

The word *stress* is used in a variety of ways in our language. According to *Webster's Ninth New Collegiate Dictionary*, stress refers to "a force exerted when one body or body part presses on, pulls on, pushes against, or tends to compress or twist another body. . . ." In the world of mechanics, stress refers to the load-bearing ability of metals. Sometimes, such pressure can actually strengthen the metal. But when the stress becomes too great, the metal fails. Thus, stress in and of itself is not bad. In fact, stress can produce some benefits, as long as its intensity and displacement are controlled.

The same is true of stress in our lives. Some stress is healthy. For example, recent studies have shown that in times of stress the pituitary gland releases a substance called beta-endorphin into our system. Beta-endorphin is a natural opiate that blocks the perception of pain in our brain. But this substance also appears to have a dramatic impact on the immune system. Over the last decade, studies have shown that beta-endorphin strengthens the power of special cells in the immune system called "natural killer cells." These cells circulate in the blood, keeping a check on tumor cells. Dr. John Morely, professor of geriatrics at the St. Louis University School of Medicine, believes that both physical and mental stress are directly responsible for the release of beta-endorphin, which in turn, enhances the potency of these natural killer cells. Thus, some stress can actually reduce the growth of tumors—as long as such stress is kept under control. Dr. Morely says, "The stress that you adequately cope with may be good for you, whereas stress that you fail to cope with . . . is most probably bad for you. Short bursts of stress are OK. Long bursts could be a problem."[3]

Look again closely at what the doctor said: Prolonged stress or stress that is not adequately dealt with can be harmful. What are the hazards of prolonged or ignored stress? First, consider the physical dangers of stress. We are all aware of the relationship between stress and high blood pressure. But new studies are demonstrating a relationship between stress and high cholesterol levels, which can cause both heart disease and a breakdown in our immune system. Dr. Robert A. Good, former head of the Memorial Sloan-Kettering Cancer Center, has pioneered research demonstrating the link between high cholesterol and immune system deficiencies:

Until the 1980s, most physicians associated abnormally high levels of cholesterol solely with diet. More recent research, however, has established a connection between emotional stress or physical fatigue and abnormally high cholesterol. . . . High cholesterol levels have been found in accountants approaching IRS deadlines, or in medical students approaching examinations. High cholesterol counts, whether from food or emotional stress, can represent an invitation to heart attacks, but, as Dr. Good and his associates have found, they can be a portal for a wide range of other illnesses as well, since a heavy burden of fat can do damage to the immune system.[4]

Such immune system deficiencies can result in cancer. Norman Cousins detailed the link between stress and disease in his book *Head First: The Biology of Hope:* "Emotional stress may contribute to the incidence of cancer by directly causing abnormal cell development or by indirectly diminishing immune surveillance or competence."[5]

Prolonged stress can also affect our emotional health. Stress causes a reaction within the body called corticotropin-releasing factor, or CRF, which causes the release of cortisol. Over a period of time, elevated cortisol levels can alter one's brain chemistry and result in chronic depression.[6]

Stress can have both positive and negative effects on our spiritual health, as well. The Bible speaks of the spiritual benefits of pressure: "Consider it all joy, my brethren, when you encounter various trials, knowing that the testing of your faith produces endurance. And let endurance have its perfect result, that you may be perfect and complete, lacking in nothing" (James 1:2-4).

The word translated "testing" is *dokimion.* The Greeks used this word to refer to a piece of pottery that had been fired in an oven. The purpose of the oven was to strengthen the pottery, not to break it. If the piece of pottery survived the oven without breaking, the potter would write the word *dokimos* on the bottom of the pottery, meaning "approved." James says that God allows stressful situations to strengthen us, not to destroy us. Such stress can have beneficial results in our relationship with God, *if we respond correctly to it.*

A friend of mine who manages a fast-food restaurant had for months been in a stress-filled situation with his assistant manager. The assistant was constantly going behind his back and complaining to the owner of the store. The manager told me that one day he was so overwhelmed by the pressure of the situation that he cried out to God, "Why would You put me in a situation where I have to pray every five minutes just to survive?" He realized he had answered his own question. God was using this stressful situation to draw that manager closer to Himself and to demonstrate His power in providing a miraculous solution to the problem. After a few months, the owner moved the assistant manager to another store. Stress can draw us closer to God.

But stress, if not handled correctly, can negatively impact our spiritual lives. Consider the example of Moses. Frustrated over the Egyptians' mistreatment of the Israelites and the slowness of God's promise of deliverance, Moses lashed out in anger, killing an Egyptian. That wrong response to stress resulted in a forty-year exile in the wilderness.

Or, look at Jonah. God commanded this prophet to travel to Nineveh to deliver an unpopular message to the Assyrians. Knowing the Assyrians' reputation for cruelty, Jonah's answer to this understandably stressful situation was to run away from God. Wrong responses to stress continue to drive people away from God. Narcotics, illicit relationships, and materialism are just some of the psuedo-escapes from stress that separate people from the ultimate answer to stress.

To summarize, some stress is good for us. But prolonged stress, or stress that is not handled properly can severely damage us physically, emotionally, and spiritually. The solution to the stress-mess is two-fold: 1. removing *unnecessary* stress and 2. dealing positively with *unavoidable* stress.

■ *Causes of Unnecessary Stress*
While it is true that all stress cannot (and should not) be removed, there are some unnecessary types of stress that I

believe are especially harmful — harmful because they tend to be prolonged and, therefore, become internalized.

1. *Stress caused by lack of purpose.* The French critic and philosopher Nicola Boileau said, "He is most fatigued who knows not what to do." We tend to stereotype goal-oriented people as consistently uptight, while the unambitious, live-for-today, person is care-free. But, in fact, the opposite is often true. Those who have never developed a life purpose, along with the resulting objectives and goals to achieve that purpose, are more prone to stress than those who have clearly defined goals. Why? A lack of purpose in life causes a person to be a victim, rather than a shaper, of circumstances.

For example, have you ever been on a trip in your car and suddenly realized you were lost? Talk about stress! And then there is that sudden surge of relief when you regain your bearings. A clearly defined life purpose is a compass that gives direction in times of uncertainty.

2. *Stress caused by unrealistic goals.* The flip-side of having no goals is having the wrong goals. Unrealistic goals or expectations can manufacture needless stress in every area of life. For example, consider the self-employed person who sets an unusually high quota for himself for the coming year. True, such goals can be motivating. But they can also become counter-productive if they produce stress instead of revenue.

When I signed a contract for my first book, the publisher gave me six months to complete it. However, in a moment of zeal that bordered on insanity, I decided to try to finish the book in three months. The only problem was that it was during this time that our first child was born. Yet, I was determined to meet the artificial deadline I had imposed. The result was needless stress in our household and a severe case of burn-out after the project was completed.

Unrealistic goals extend into other areas of our lives as well. Some people, trying to juggle a hectic work schedule with the demands of raising of family, still try to keep their homes looking like a builder's model. Others place unrealistic scholastic or athletic expectations on their children. Such expectations infect an entire family with needless stress.

Even vacations can produce stress—when they are weighed down with the baggage of unrealistic goals. Tim Hansel gives this word of warning about vacations:

> Since they've waited fifty weeks for this vacation, some people try to cram a year's worth of living into two weeks. They wind up pushing harder and spending longer hours than they do on the job. Rushing from one place to the next, "hurrying up to be happy," it's no wonder that peace eludes them. . . . Related to this image that vacation is a reward for hard work is the notion that therefore we are supposed to enjoy this time, and if we don't, we feel anxious. We carry so many bionic images of leisure into the vacation that nothing could ever match it— and then wonder why we're so unhappy.[7]

3. Stress caused by unresolved anger. Closely related to unrealistic goals as a cause of stress is the problem of anger. Anger is the negative emotion we feel when our expectations are not met. Those unmet expectations may range from a traffic light not changing quickly enough to our spouse not giving us the attention we feel we deserve. Such unresolved anger can be deadly. The relationship between hostility and an imbalance in the endocrine system of our bodies is well-documented. Anger decreases the lymphocytes in our bodies, which results in decreased antibodies to ward off infectious diseases. In their book *Happiness is a Choice*, Christian psychiatrists Frank Minirth and Paul Meier make this bold assertion: "Pent-up anger is probably the leading cause of death."[8]

That is why the Word of God commands us to be "quick to hear, slow to speak, and slow to anger" (James 1:19). The Greek word used for anger is the word *orge*, which refers to a smoldering, persistent anger, rather than a temporary outburst. James makes it clear that such long-term anger is not of God: "For the anger of man does not achieve the righteousness of God" (1:20).

Is anger always wrong? Not necessarily. But anger is like a fever—it is usually an indication that something else is wrong—either in our attitudes or in our relationships. The Apostle Paul said, "Be angry, and yet do not sin; do not let the sun go down on your anger, and do not give the devil an opportunity" (Eph. 4:26-27). In other words, deal with your anger before it destroys you.

4. *Stress caused by comparison to others.* My friend Howard Hendricks calls comparison the favorite indoor sport among Christians. We love to compare our homes, our families, our vocational achievements, our bank accounts, and our appearances to those around us. But such comparison is a sure-fire way to produce discontent and stress. (More will be said about it in the next chapter "Choosing Contentment over Comparison.")

5. *Stress caused by materialism.* There seems to be an inseparable link between materialism and stress. Remember the parable that Jesus told in Luke 12 about the rich man who enjoyed very productive land? He had more than enough money to meet his needs. Yet he was not content to enjoy the blessings of God. Instead, he was obsessed about building larger barns to store his increasing produce. Materialism causes stress. The more we have, the more we worry. That is why the writer of Ecclesiastes observed, "The abundance of a rich man permits him no sleep" (Ecc. 5:12, NIV). Unfortunately, this farmer did not have to worry about his "problem" for long. God took his life, forcing the farmer to leave everything behind.

By the way, you don't have to be rich to be stressed out over money. Materialism is based on our attitude toward money, not the amount of money we possess. Materialism is the conviction that money or possessions can satisfy our deepest needs. And the poor are just as susceptible to that illusion as the rich—in fact, they are sometimes more susceptible to it, since they have never experienced wealth.

Jesus closed His story about the farmer with these words: "For this reason I say to you, do not be anxious [stressed-out] for your life, as to what you shall eat; nor for your body, as to what you shall put on. For life is more than food, and the body than clothing (Luke 12:22-23).

6. *Stress caused by physical fatigue.* Physical exhaustion distorts our perception of reality. The fatigued individ-

ual is prone to stress and depression. Remember the story of Elijah? After his exhilarating victory at Mt. Carmel, he found himself fleeing from Queen Jezebel. After the 120-mile run from Jezreel to Beersheba, Elijah broke under the stress: "But he himself went a day's journey into the wilderness, and came and sat down under a juniper tree; and he requested for himself that he might die, and said, 'It is enough; now, O Lord, take my life, for I am not better than my fathers' " (1 Kings 19:4).

Elijah's fear of Jezebel was not based on reality. Why should he fear Jezebel? He had just slaughtered 850 false prophets! But physical fatigue had altered his perspective. Vince Lombardi once said, "Fatigue makes cowards of us all." Elijah had been so busy doing the work of God that he had not taken care of his physical needs—and as a result he was stressed out. Only after several days of rest and nourishment was Elijah ready to continue his service for God (see 1 Kings 19:5-9).

■ *Choosing Relaxation Over Stress*

While some stress is unnecessary, other types of stress are unavoidable—stress that comes from work, family, or just the minor irritations of everyday life. How do you handle the inevitable problems of life? The basic thrust of this book is that our lives are defined by the attitude choices we make. And one of the clearest choices we make in life is how to deal with unavoidable stress. Remember the definition of an attitude? "Attitudes are our mental and emotional responses to the circumstances of life." When I write about "choosing relaxation" over stress, I am not referring to an escapist mentality that refuses to confront real problems. Nor am I suggesting some superficial solutions that fail to deal with the root causes of stress. Instead, I am speaking of meeting the root causes of stress head-on and developing appropriate mental, emotional, and spiritual reponses to those stresses. Relaxation is not as much an activity as it is an attitude. How can you develop an attitude of relaxation?

1. *Gain God's perspective on problems.* Stress is an attitude that initially results in our responding to problems

with panic. But an attitude of relaxation responds to problems with expectation. "Consider it all joy, my brethren, when you encounter various trials" (James 1:2). James says that our first response to unavoidable stress should be joy. I don't think James is speaking about giddiness—that is a bit unrealistic. ("Oh boy, the car battery is dead! How exciting!") Instead, I believe James is referring to a calm assurance that God is in control of the situation. He is saying that Christians can respond gracefully to stress. In fact, the words *joy* and *grace* come from the same root word in Greek.

Why can we respond that way to problems? Because "the testing of your faith produces endurance" (v. 3). In other words, James is saying that problems are opportunities for us to grow. The Greek root of the word *problem* means "to drive or thrust forward." Problems thrust us forward in our spiritual growth.

2. *Live life in the present tense.* When we spend our time dwelling on mistakes we have made in the past (which we can't change) or anticipating problems in the future (which we can't foresee), we are prone to stress. And we are robbed of the joy of the present moment. It is interesting that in the Old Testament the most holy name for God is translated "I Am." And throughout the Gospel of John Jesus refers to Himself as "I Am." The following piece by Helen Mallicoat reminds us of the significance of that truth in our lives:

I was regretting the past and fearing the future.
Suddenly my Lord was speaking to me.
"My name is I AM."
He paused. I waited. He continued.
"When you live in the past, with its mistakes and regrets, it is hard. I am not there. My name is not I WAS."
"When you live in the future, with its problems and fears, it is hard. I am not there. My name is not I WILL BE."
"When you live in this moment, it is not hard. I am here. My name is I AM."[9]

3. *Take a day off every week.* I can just hear some of you right now. "That's easy for you preachers to say. You work only one hour a week! But if you had my job, you know that would be impossible." The fact is that one of God's earliest commands was to rest one day a week. In the Old Testament, such a day was known as the Sabbath. The Sabbath was more than just a day of worship—it was a day of rest, patterned after God's own work schedule:

> Six days you shall labor and do all your work, but the seventh day is a Sabbath of the Lord your God; in it you shall not do any work, you or your son or your daughter. . . . For in six days the Lord made the heavens and the earth, and the sea and all that is in them, and rested on the seventh day; therefore the Lord blessed the Sabbath Day and made it holy (Ex. 20:9-11).

Man was not made to work seven days a week. Such an unrealistic schedule is guaranteed to produce stress and burn-out. Obviously, God did not *need* a day of rest. He did not finish the work of creation and say, "Whew, this has worn Me out! I need a break!!" Instead, God was setting a pattern for the way we should work. We *do* need a day of rest to replenish our physical, emotional, and spiritual resources.

Let me sound a word of caution here. A day of rest should not be confused with a day of recreation. In the Old Testament, the Sabbath was a day, first of all, of worship. Even Jesus, the Son of God, saw the importance of gathering together with other believers for worship. Part of His schedule was a regular day of worship: "And He came to Nazareth, where He had been brought up, *and as was His custom,* He entered the synagogue on the Sabbath" (Luke 4:16).

Tragically, we preachers have turned the Christian day of worship into an endurance contest. One layman commented, "I'm sure glad that there is only one rest day per week; I'd burn out if we had to go through two 'days of rest' like this every seven days."[10]

Secondly, a day of rest is also a time to regain perspective as we meditate on God and His work in our lives. Few people have ever possessed the zeal and energy of the Christian abolitionist William Wilberforce. Yet Sunday served as a balm for the stress in his life. In his journal he wrote, "Blessed be to God for the day of rest and religious occupation wherein earthly things assume their true size. Ambition is stunted."[11]

4. *Spend some time every day doing something you enjoy.* Everyone needs something to look forward to — every day. In his book *Beware the Naked Man Who Offers You His Shirt*, Harvey Mackay asks, "How do you overcome the inevitable drag on your spirits of doing tasks you hate but that have to be done? . . . If I have to do something I don't like, I make it a point to be especially nice to myself later by doing something I really do like. The same day."[11]

Sundays really are an endurance contest for me. Preaching two different messages, committee meetings, hosting a radio program, and listening to the complaints people have been waiting all week to dump on me make for a stress-filled day. But at the end of the evening, I reward myself with a large bowl of popcorn, a giant Diet Coke, and an old movie. I'll admit this doesn't sound very spiritual, but the way I make it through the day is by eagerly anticipating the end of the day, when I know I will be able to relax.

Just knowing that you are going to get to spend a few minutes doing something *you* want to do — a hobby, a sport, reading a book, watching a television program — can help relieve the stress of the day.

5. *Spend time with God each day.* In my own life, I have discovered that the way I begin and end each day greatly affects my stress level. It is impossible to effectively manage stress without spending time with the One who offers the ultimate solution to stress. That is why I have adopted Lloyd Ogilvie's personal devotional plan called "Fifteen Minutes to Freedom." This pastor suggests spending fifteen minutes at the beginning of each day and the same amount of time at the end of each day in a combination of prayer, Bible reading, and thanksgiving to God.

I believe that Jesus' secret to "overcoming the world"

was in the amount of time He spent with God. Jesus refused to allow His many responsibilities to keep Him from spending time with His Father. I have always been fascinated with Mark 1:35: "And in the early morning, while it was still dark, He arose and went out and departed to a lonely place, and was praying there." As you examine the context of this verse, you will find that this was one of the busiest days in Jesus' entire ministry—yet, He began the day on His knees. To Jesus, time spent with God was not just another religious requirement; it was the secret of His strength and the source of His tranquility.

And God offers the same strength and tranquility in the midst of a stress-filled life to you:

He gives strength to the weary, and to him who lacks might He increases power. Though youths grow weary and tired, and vigorous young men stumble badly, yet those who wait for the Lord will gain new strength; they will mount up with wings like eagles, they will run and not get tired, they will walk and not become weary" (Isaiah 40:29-31).

CHAPTER SEVEN

CHOOSING CONTENTMENT OVER COMPARISON

"Not that I speak from want; for I have learned to be content in whatever circumstances I am. I know how to get along with humble means, and I also know how to live in prosperity; in any and every circumstance I have learned the secret of being filled and going hungry, both of having abundance and suffering need."   Phil. 4:11-12.

■ The recent revival of the old TV game show "Let's Make a Deal" reminds me of an important lesson I learned about the foolishness of comparison and the joy of contentment. It was TV's big dealer himself, Monty Hall, who helped enlighten me.

A few years ago, my wife and I were vacationing with some friends in California and heard that the game show "Let's Make a Deal" was looking for some contestants to try out for the next day's episode. We quickly went to the nearest costume shop to select some crazy-looking outfits that would perhaps get us on the program. After all, we were told, the competition would be stiff. We didn't care if we won any money or not—all we wanted was to be able to say that we had been on the show. After selecting our costumes, we headed for the studio.

Much to our surprise, we were chosen to be on the show, and it wasn't long into the show until Monty approached me (I was dressed in a full-length banana costume) and said, "Robert Jeffress, my next deal is for you!" I ended up winning $350. Then, Monty went to my friends, and they won $1,200.

When the show was over, we were taken to a small room to fill out some information about ourselves and sign the necessary releases. While sitting in that room, I began wishing I would have won the piano that the woman sitting next to me had traded something else for. If only I had been in that seat. My friends started lamenting that they had not gone for the Big Deal of the Day, instead of keeping the $1,200. And the woman who won the Big Deal of the Day complained that some of the furniture would not match the decor of her living room.

Above all the winners' moaning and lamenting, I heard one contestant say, "I'm just glad I even got on the program. I wasn't expecting anything." At that moment, I began to clearly see the foolishness of comparison and the elusiveness of contentment.[1] I thought of Benjamin Franklin's observation, "Who is rich? He that is content. Who is that? Nobody."

Nothing steals our happiness more than comparison. And yet we continually compare ourselves with other people. I don't mean simply observing, for example, there are people who possess more than we do—better homes, finer cars, fatter portfolios, more attractive appearances.

Nor does comparison mean an appreciation of the finer things in life. There is nothing inherently sinful about admiring what someone else has. The Word of God reminds us that "every good thing bestowed and every perfect gift is from above, coming down from the Father of lights" (James 1:17).

Nor should comparison be confused with the innate desire we all have to excel. In the next chapter we will contrast the God-given desire to produce with the attitude of slothfulness. Such productivity is often the result of a desire to have more. That desire is not necessarily evil, as long as it is within the framework of God's will for us.

Then what *is* comparison? It is an attitude of dissatisfaction with God's provisions for my life that leads to an obsession with having more. In the Old Testament, such an attitude was called covetousness. The tenth commandment was a prohibition against developing this attitude: "You shall not covet your neighbor's house; you shall not covet your neighbor's wife or his male servant or his female servant or his ox or his donkey or anything that belongs to your neighbor" (Ex. 20:17).

The danger of such an obsession is that it often leads to idolatry, adultery, theft, and murder. The relationship between coveting and sin is clearly seen in both the Old and New Testaments. The prophet Micah demonstrated the relationship between covetousness and theft:

> Woe to those who scheme iniquity, who work out evil on their beds! When morning comes, they do it, for it is in the power of their hands. They covet fields and then seize them, and houses, and take them away. They rob a man and his house, and a man and his inheritance (Micah 2:1-2).

I believe that the commandment against covetousness is the climax of the decalogue. It represents the origin of all sin—the mind. Idolatry, a failure to reverence God, working instead of worshiping, dishonoring one's parents, murder, adultery, theft, and lying are the natural by-products of dissatisfaction that stems from comparison.

In fact, when you examine the origin of sin in the world, you will find the root problem was comparison. Satan was a member of the highest angelic order. He had vast responsibilities over God's creation. But he was not content with the position God had given him. Instead, he started comparing himself with God. And as he compared himself with His Creator, sin entered his heart: "But you said in your heart, 'I will ascend to heaven; I will raise my throne above the stars of God, and I will sit on the mount of assembly in the recesses of the north. I will ascend above the heights of the clouds; I will make myself like the Most High' " (Is. 14:13-14).

Interestingly, Satan tempted Eve with the same sin that had caused his own downfall—a desire to be like God. Satan was successful in causing Eve to be discontent with her position in God's creation and enticed her with the promise that she could have more—in fact, she could be like God: "For God knows that in the day you eat from it your eyes will be opened, and you will be like God, knowing good and evil" (Gen. 3:5).

Satan has not changed his strategy. And why should he? By perpetuating the myth of "more," he has been successful in causing continual chaos in peoples' lives. For example, Lot's desire for more productive land caused him to settle in Sodom. Jacob's desire for more inheritance led him to cheat his brother Esau. Joseph's brothers' desire for more attention caused Joseph to be sold into slavery. Moses' desire for a more hasty end to the Israelite's slavery caused him to kill the Egyptian soldier. David's desire for a more thrilling sex life led him into adultery with Bathsheba. Solomon's desire for more wealth, pleasure, and power caused him to turn away from God—and on and on and on.

And we see the same scenes being played out today. A professing Christian making $125,000 a year is caught embezzelling less than $100 a week out of petty cash and loses his job. He wanted more.

A Christian wife and mother begins "innocently" flirting with a married man. Soon it erupts into a full-blown affair. In the process she loses her husband, and ultimately, her lover. She wanted more.

A pastor, desiring to have the largest and finest church sanctuary in his denomination, shares his "vision from God" with his church. Borrowing heavily for construction, the church eventually finds it cannot make the debt payments and continue its program. The church teeters on the brink of insolvency. All because the pastor wanted more.

What is tragic about each of these situations is that "more" ends up becoming less. Instead of more income, the businessman now has no income. Instead of having someone else to love her, the woman now has no one to love her. Instead of a bigger church, the pastor now has no church. That is the deception of Satan. Jesus was right when he referred to Satan as a "liar and the father of lies" (John 8:44).

I have prided myself on my business acumen—I majored in business in college and have learned to handle money well. Yet I will admit that I have made two terrible investments in my lifetime. And in both cases, a burning desire for *more* eclipsed sound judgment. In the first case, a silver commodities trader explained to me how I could "control $50,000 worth of silver for only $5,000!" Of course, what he did not explain was that anytime there is a potential for great gain there is the equal and greater possibility of tremendous loss. Guess what I experienced?

My second blunder occurred when a deacon wanted to help me become a millionaire through no-money down real estate investing. Fortunately, I purchased only a few properties. But some members of the church, intent on becoming full-fledged real estate moguls, purchased many properties and ended up declaring bankruptcy. All because of a desire for *more*. As we will see in the next chapter, there is nothing wrong with investments. But if the investment is built on greed, the result will be disaster.

■ The Problems with Comparison

What is wrong with comparing ourselves to other people? Comparison leads to covetousness, the root of almost all sin. But the problem with comparison is not only the disastrous results it produces, but also the faulty assumptions that cause us to want to compare ourselves with others. What are those wrong assumptions?

Myth #1: "This is America—I can have it all!" The so-called "American dream" is that there is no limit to what you can achieve if you so desire. You can have the highest income, the finest education, the biggest house, the most attractive spouse, if you just work hard enough.

Now, here is a lesson from Reality 101. There will always be someone who has more than you do! For example, you have probably seen those lists of the 100 wealthiest people in the world. Ninety-nine of those people are probably dissatisfied because there is someone who has more than they do. And the one person who is at the top of the list probably longs for something that one of the other ninety-nine has.

In a sermon called "Rare and Remarkable Virtues," Bill Hybels, pastor of Willow Creek Community Church in South Barrington, Illinois, recounted the tragic story of Howard Hughes:

> All he ever really wanted in life was more. He wanted more money, so he parlayed inherited wealth into a billion-dollar pile of assets. He wanted more fame, so he broke into the Hollywood scene and soon became a filmmaker and star. He wanted more sensual pleasures, so he paid handsome sums to indulge his every sexual urge. He wanted more thrills, so he designed, built, and piloted the fastest aircraft in the world. He wanted more power, so he secretly dealt political favors so skillfully that two U.S. presidents became his pawns. All he ever wanted was more.... [Yet he died] emaciated, color-less, with his fingernails in grotesque, inches-long cork-screws; with rotting black teeth, tumors, and innumera-ble needle marks from his drug addiction. Howard Hughes died believing the myth of "more."

Myth #2: "I could really be happy if only I had . . ."
Whenever we think that anyone or anything other than God can satisfy our deepest needs, we have become guilty of idolatry. People will fill in the above blank with all kinds of responses—prestige, a larger home, time off from work, or sensual pleasure. But probably the most common response to the above statement is "money." If only I had more money, I could be happy." The Bible makes it clear that the desire for money is the root cause for covetousness and many other sins: "For the love of money is a root of all sorts of evil, and some by longing for it have wandered away from the faith, and pierced themselves with many a pang" (1 Tim. 6:10).

There is a two-fold problem with idols, such as money. First, they divert our attention from God ("no man can

serve two masters"). But also, they are incapable of fulfilling our needs. The psalmist reminds us that those who turn
to their idols in times of trouble are doomed to
disappointment:

> Their idols are silver and gold, the work of man's
> hands. They have mouths, but they cannot speak; they
> have eyes, but they cannot see; they have ears, but
> they cannot hear; they have noses, but they cannot
> smell; they have hands, but they cannot feel; they
> have feet but they cannot walk; they cannot make a
> sound with their throat. Those who make them will
> become like them, everyone who trusts in them (Ps.
> 115:4-7).

Why can't money satisfy our needs? The wealthiest man
of his day provided these observations about the futility of
wealth:

> Whoever loves money never has money enough; who-
> ever loves wealth is never satisfied with his income.
> This too is meaningless. As goods increase, so do
> those who consume them. And what benefit are they
> to the owner except to feast his eyes on them? The
> sleep of a laborer is sweet, whether he eats little or
> much, but the abundance of a rich man permits him
> no sleep. I have seen a grievous evil under the sun:
> wealth hoarded to the harm of its owner, or wealth
> lost through some misfortune. . . . Naked a man
> comes from his mother's womb, and as he comes so
> he departs. He takes nothing from his labor that he
> can carry in his hand (Ecc. 5:10-15, NIV).

Notice the six reasons Solomon says money cannot
satisfy:

1. *No one ever has enough money (5:10).* You have
heard of Parkinson's Law: "Work expands to fill the available time." Let me give you a variation of that law—I call it
Jeffress' Law—"Expenses expand to fill the available income." I hear couples lament, "We are making more mon-

ey now than we have ever made in our lives, and yet where does it all go?" No matter how much money you make, it will never seem to be enough.

2. *Money attracts parasites (5:11)*. As Solomon looked at the palace payroll, he noticed all kinds of bodyguards, servants, concubines, and accountants who were consuming his wealth. Who *are* these people? The same phenomenon is true today: the more you have, the more people there are to consume your income—family members, employees, and the Internal Revenue Service.

3. *Money produces anxiety (5:12)*. We saw in the last chapter that wealth can produce stress. Solomon observed that the common laborer punches in at eight and out at five. He is able to come home, eat dinner, read the paper, go to a Little League game, watch the news, and go to bed. Compare that simple existence to the complex life of those who own their own businesses or are in a managerial position. They worry about sales figures, payrolls, employee problems, government regulations, and a myriad of other concerns. Great wealth can be a great headache!

4. *Money can be harmful (5:13)*. Solomon, probably speaking from personal experience, observed that hoarding money can be dangerous to one's emotional and spiritual health. How? Hoarding money can rob us of present joy in life. You likely have encountered people who are always "saving for a rainy day." They continually postpone pleasure, choosing instead to stockpile their money so that they might be protected from every possible adverse circumstance in life. I like the sage wisdom of Dolly Levi, the lead character in the musical "Hello Dolly" who said something to the effect: "Money is a lot like manure; pile it in one place and it begins to stink; but spread it around and it does some good."

But money that is hoarded can also rob a person of eternal life. It was the love of money that caused

the rich farmer to deceive himself in thinking all was well;
the rich young ruler to reject Christ;
the rich man to neglect Lazarus;

Judas to betray the Lord Jesus Christ;
Ananias and Saphira to lie to the Holy Spirit.

5. *Money can be easily lost (5:14).* How tragic it is to
sacrifice and save all of your life, only to lose your money
through an investment scam or a catastrophic illness. Realizing how easily wealth can be lost, Solomon offered this
advice: "Do not wear yourself out to get rich; have the
wisdom to show restraint. Cast but a glance at riches, and
they are gone, for they will surely sprout wings and fly off
to the sky like an eagle" (Prov. 23:4-5, NIV).

6. *Money is only temporal (5:15).* Solomon reminds us
in verses 15–17 that God does not allow any U-Hauls in
heaven. You came into this world with nothing and you will
leave with nothing. The following letter to Ann Landers
illustrates the old maxim: "You can't take it with you":

> Aunt "Emma" was married to a tightwad who was
> also a little strange. He made a good salary, but they
> lived frugally because he insisted on putting 20 per-
> cent of his paycheck under the mattress. . . . The
> money, he said, was going to come in handy in their
> old age.
>
> When "Uncle Ollie" was sixty, he was stricken with
> cancer. Toward the end, he made Aunt Emma prom-
> ise, in the presence of his brothers, that she would put
> the money he had stashed away in his coffin so he
> could buy his way into heaven if he had to.
>
> They all knew he was a little odd, but this was clear-
> ly a crazy request. Aunt Em did promise, however,
> and assured Uncle Ollie's brothers that she was a
> woman of her word and would do as he asked.
>
> The following morning she took the money (about
> $26,000) to the bank and deposited it. She then wrote
> a check and put it in the coffin four days later.[2]

The limitations that prevent money from satisfying our
deepest desires are present in every other idol that man
has ever erected—power, pleasure, relationships, work,
achievement, etc.

If, indeed, there will always be people with more of something than we have, and if those things cannot ultimately satisfy us anyway, what is the secret to lasting happiness? In a word . . . contentment.

Contentment is an attutude that says, "I will be satisfied with what God has given me." Contentment should not be confused with complacency. The Apostle Paul was always content with what he had, but never with what he was. Paul was always striving to be more like Christ: "I press on toward the goal for the prize of the upward call of God in Christ Jesus" (Phil. 3:14).

Contentment can best be understood by examining its etymological root. The word *contentment* comes from a word that means "containment." It describes a person who is "self-contained"—that is, he is able to derive satisfaction from his inner resources, rather than from external sources. To the Christian, of course, that inner resource is a relationship to Christ. Such a resource allows the content person to be happy, regardless of his circumstances. Consider again the Apostle Paul. As he sat in a damp Roman prison, awaiting what could have been his execution, he penned these words:

I have learned to be content in whatever circumstances I am. I know how to get along with humble means, and I also know how to live in prosperity; in any and every circumstance I have learned the secret of being filled and going hungry, both of having abundance and suffering need. I can do all things through Him who strengthens me" (Phil. 4:11-13).

What is "the secret" that allows a person to be content? Here are three keys to contentment:

Key #1: Compare yourself to God's standard rather than human standards of success. Paul knew what it was like to live in the rat race. He had been one of those super achievers who was determined to be the best at everything. As a successful Jew, he had been determined to keep up with the Jonesbergs! Yet once he became a Christian, he realized that all of his achievements were worthless—all that mattered was God's approval: "But whatever things were gain to me, those things I have counted as loss for the sake of Christ. More than that, I count all things to be loss in view of the surpassing value of knowing Christ Jesus my Lord" (Phil. 3:7-8).

The great Baptist pastor George W. Truett gave the best definition of true success I have ever heard: "Success is knowing the will of God and doing it." When you stand before the judgment seat of Christ, the Lord will not ask you if you were successful in accomplishing great evangelistic crusades. No, God will only judge you according to the opportunities He gave *you* to serve Him.

Key #2: Trust in God's sovereign plan for your life. Do you realize that the most important aspects of your life were predetermined by God: your parents, your heredity, your emotional makeup, along with dozens of other factors? The psalmist wrote,

> You made all the delicate, inner parts of my body, and then knit them together in my mother's womb. Thank you for making me so wonderfully complex! It is amazing to think about. Your workmanship is marvelous—and how well I know it. You were there while I was being formed in utter seclusion! You saw me before I was born and scheduled each day of my life before I began to breathe. Every day was recorded in your book! (Ps. 139:13-15, TLB).

If God has a unique blueprint for all those areas of your life, is it too much to believe that His plan also includes other details of your life: your vocation, your spouse, your children, your income? In the next chapter, we will see that we do have responsibility for managing our resources well. But to a large degree, God has predetermined our economic status in life. Look at Elihu's description of God, recorded in Job 34:19: "Who shows no partiality to princes nor regards the rich above the poor, for they are all the work of His hands."

That truth is the basis for Paul's instruction to Timothy regarding the wealthy: "Instruct those who are rich in this present world not to be conceited or to fix their hope on the uncertainty of riches, but on God, who richly supplies us with all things to enjoy" (1 Tim. 6:17). We should neither be conceited nor despondent over our bank accounts. Why? Because ultimately it is God who supplies our money — and He does so according to His eternal and *unique* plan for our lives.

Key #3: Limit your expectations. A man went up and down his block passing out $100 bills to every household for no reason other than his generosity. He did this day after day for an entire month. One day, he inadvertently missed a house. The owner of the house stuck his head out the window and violently cursed the man for not delivering his $100 bill.

Many of us are like that in our relationship with God. We have a list of "basic expectations" that are based on what God has given us in the past, or what He has given someone else. And such a list of expectations is one of the greatest enemies of contentment. A crucial key to contentment is shortening our expectation list and thanking God for anything beyond that list.

Paul reminded Timothy of the importance of limited expectations: "For we have brought nothing into the world, so we cannot take anything out of it either. And if we have food and covering, with these we shall be content" (1 Tim. 6:7-8). According to Paul, then, if you have more than food and covering, you are ahead of the game.

At the beginning of this book, we learned than an attitude is a response to the circumstances of life. How do you respond to the inevitable situation of someone else having more than you have? You can respond by comparison — which is a nice term for covetousness and leads to certain sin. Or you can be content. To develop an attitude of contentment, remember:

1. God's plan for your life is unique; therefore, refuse to compare yourself with others.

2. God's purpose for your life is based on His elective will; therefore, trust in His sovereignty.

3. God's provisions for your life come from His goodness; therefore, be grateful for what He has *already* provided.[3]

CHAPTER EIGHT

CHOOSING FORGIVENESS OVER BITTERNESS

"And be kind to one another, tender-hearted, forgiving each other, just as God in Christ also has forgiven you."   *Eph. 4:32*

■ "What is the worst sin a Christian can commit?" That is a question I am occasionally asked in my weekly newspaper column "Ask the Doctor." Ask other Christians the same question and you will get a variety of responses. Among the top-vote getters will be murder, adultery, homosexuality, incest, and divorce. Of course, we know from a theological perspective that God does not grade sin. The smallest infraction of God's law is equated with breaking all of God's laws (see James 2:10). In fact, God makes no distinction between sins of the mind and sins of the flesh. Jesus made it clear that if we hate someone in our heart it is tantamount to murder; if a man lusts after a woman in his heart, it is tantamount to adultery.

And yet there are obviously some sins that have greater consequences than others. Hatred may be equal to murder in God's eyes, but that emotion alone has never sent anyone to the electric chair. Few homes have been destroyed solely because of a fleeting lustful thought, but many families are torn apart because of adultery. Yes, some sins *do* have greater consequences than others.

However, at the top of my list for the most destructive of all sins is not murder, adultery, or any of the other "Big Five." Bitterness wins the award hands down. In my experience as a pastor, I have seen bitterness destroy more people, families, and churches than those other sins combined.

What is bitterness? In this book, I have defined attitudes as our mental and emotional responses to the circumstances of life. One circumstance that we all frequently encounter is being treated unjustly. Our mistreatment may come from a family member who wrongs us, a friend who betrays us, an employer who falsely accuses us, a church that ignores us, or a God who disappoints us. It is difficult to go through a day without being offended! And with each offense comes a clear choice. We can choose to forgive the offender, or we can choose not to forgive. Bitterness is an attitude that refuses to forgive offenses. And bitterness, like a cancer, grows and grows until it destroys everything around it. That is why the writer of Hebrews warned, "See to it that no one comes short of the grace of God; that no root of bitterness springing up causes trouble, and by it many be defiled" (12:15).

On the other hand, forgiveness is an attitude that honestly acknowledges an offense and then dismisses it on the basis of God's forgiveness of us. The Greek word often used in the Bible for forgiveness means "to release." What a clear picture of forgiveness! Bitterness holds on to an offense; forgiveness releases it. And such a release is absolutely necessary for our physical, emotional, and spiritual health. How can we let go of an offense that has scarred us deeply? First, we need to understand the biblical basis for forgiveness.

■ *A Tale of Two Debtors.*
The Apostle Peter once asked Jesus, "Lord, how often shall my brother sin against me and I forgive him? Up to seven times?" (Matt. 18:21). Previously in Matthew 18, Jesus had been discussing church discipline. Jesus made it clear that before a sinning believer could be allowed back into the fellowship of the church, that sinner must first

repent. But Peter's question changed the subject. No longer was Jesus talking about sins against the church; He now spoke about personal offenses—notice Peter's words "sin against *me.*"

How often should I forgive someone who wrongs me? The rabbis taught three times was sufficient. So Peter thought he was being quite magnanimous by offering to forgive seven times. But Jesus was not impressed. "I do not say to you, up to seven times, but up to seventy times seven" (18:22). Jesus was not saying that offense #491 did not have to be forgiven. The phrase "seventy times seven" was a Hebrew expression that denoted infinity. There is to be no limit to our willingness to forgive someone who wrongs us. Why? To answer that question Jesus told a parable:

For this reason the kingdom of heaven may be compared to a certain king who wished to settle acounts with his slaves. And when he had begun to settle them, there was brought to him one who owed him ten thousand talents. But since he did not have the means to repay, his lord commanded him to be sold, along with his wife and children and all that he had, and repayments to be made. The slave therefore falling down, prostrated himself before him, saying, "Have patience with me, and I will repay you everything." And the lord of that slave felt compassion and released him and forgave him the debt. But that slave went out and found one of his fellow slaves who owed him a hundred denarii; and he seized him and began to choke him, saying, "Pay back what you owe." So his fellow slave fell down and began to entreat him, saying, "Have patience with me and I will repay you." He was unwilling however, but went and threw him in prison until he should pay back what was owed. So when his fellow slaves saw what had happened, they were deeply grieved and came and reported to their lord all that had happened. Then summoning him, his lord said to him, "You wicked slave, I forgave you all that debt because you entreated me. Should you not also have had mercy on your fellow slave as I had mercy on you?" And his lord, moved with anger, handed him over to the torturers until he should repay all that was owed him. So shall My heavenly Father also do to you, if each of you does not forgive his brother from your heart (Matt. 18:23-35).

The reason we are to forgive other people for their sins against us is because of God's willingness to forgive us for our offenses against Him. Notice in the parable the disparity between the amounts of money owed. The first slave owed the king 10,000 talents. A talent was a standard of weight for precious metals equaling 60 to 80 pounds. If the measure was based on gold, you can see what a large sum this was! At current prices, a standard of gold was worth about $500,000. Now, multiply that by 10,000 and you see that this slave was in *big trouble!*

Besides being a debtor, this slave was also a lender. A fellow slave owed him one hundred denarii. A denarii was a Roman coin worth about sixteen cents, or a day's wage. In today's dollars, that amounts to about $16. Now remember, this is a parable. It is improbable that a slave could be in the position of owing someone five billion dollars (unless he had a terrible gambling problem!). But Jesus uses this hyperbole to illustrate the tremendous debt we owe God. Just as the king graciously forgave the slave his debt, God has forgiven us of our sins against Him.

The difference between our offenses against God and others' offenses against us is as great as the difference between $5 billion and $16. If God was willing to forgive us of our sins, should we not be willing to forgive others of their relatively insignificant offenses? That is the biblical basis for forgiveness. We forgive others on the basis of God's forgiving us. That principle is most succinctly stated in Ephesians 4:32: "And be kind to one another, tender-hearted, forgiving each other, *just as* God in Christ also has forgiven you."

Let's take a moment and examine the phrase "just as God in Christ also has forgiven you." If our interpretation of Matthew 18 and Ephesians 4 is correct, then these nine words are key to understanding how we are to forgive others. If we can discover how God forgives us, then we are able to understand how we are to forgive others. Romans 5 contains some of the clearest verses in the Bible describing God's forgiveness: "Therefore having been justified by faith, we have peace with God through our Lord Jesus Christ.... For while we were still helpless, at the right time Christ died for the ungodly.... But God demonstrates His own love toward us, in that while we were yet sinners, Christ died for us (Rom. 5:1, 6, 8).

As I read these verses, two facts become evident about God's forgiveness:

1. *God forgave us when we did not deserve forgiveness.* God forgave us "while we were yet sinners." I am always amazed at our inability to grasp this truth. Ask the average person the question, "What kind of people are going to heaven?" and typical responses will be: those who go to church, those who read their Bibles, those who love their neighbors as themselves, those who believe in God. In other words, God forgives "good" people.

While that seems logical, it is contrary to God's Word. Good people don't need forgiveness; bad people need forgiveness. Jesus spent much of His ministry illustrating that truth. He was constantly being criticized by the self-righteous Pharisees for spending time with tax-gatherers and sinners (synonymous terms both then and now!). Jesus replied to the charge with a simple observation: "It is not those who are healthy who need a physician, but those who are ill" (Matt. 9:12). Jesus was in the business of healing the unrighteous, not the righteous.

Of course, there are no truly righteous people. Both the Old and New Testaments affirm, "There is none righteous, not even one" (Ps. 14:3; Rom. 3:10). But some people cannot accept the truth, and therefore, are unable to accept God's mercy. The only difference between the Pharisees and the sinners to whom Jesus ministered was in their willingness to admit their need for forgiveness.

What the Bible is saying is that God forgave us when we least deserved it—*while we were sinners.* Paul vividly described how undeserving we were of God's forgiveness:

"And although you were formerly alienated and hostile in mind, engaged in evil deeds, yet He has now reconciled you in His fleshly body through death, in order to present you before Him holy and blameless and beyond reproach" (Col. 1:21-22). Notice the descriptions "alienated," "hostile," and "engaged in evil deeds." Like the bumper sticker says, "We are not forgiven because we are good; we are good because we are forgiven."

2. *God forgave us on the basis of grace, not works.* Nothing I do or don't do can ever earn God's forgiveness. Romans 5:1 says we are justified—declared forgiven by God—by His undeserved grace which we receive by faith. Why does God refuse to allow us to earn His forgiveness? Look at Romans 4:4-5: "Now to the one who works, his wage is not reckoned as a favor, but as what is due. But to the one who does not work, but believes in Him who justifies the ungodly, his faith is reckoned as righteousness."

When you get paid each month, what is the first thing you do? Do you go into your employer's office and thank him for such a generous and unexpected gift? Why not? Because what you received was not a gift but an obligation. You have a contract with your employer—you receive X dollars for a specified amount of work. What you receive on the fifteenth and thirtieth of each month is not a gift but an obligation.

Paul is saying that if we do anything to earn God's forgiveness, then forgiveness is not a gift but an obligation. And God absolutely refuses to owe any person forgiveness. That is why eternal life is reserved for the person "who does not work."

Now, let's review what we have learned about God's forgiveness:

1. God forgave us when we did not deserve forgiveness.
2. God forgave us on the basis of grace, not works.

Why this short theological treatise on salvation? Remember Ephesians 4:32? We are to forgive one another "just as God in Christ also has forgiven [us]." That means we are to forgive those who do not deserve to be forgiven. And secondly, we are not to require people to earn forgiveness. Such unconditional forgiveness is in direct opposition to what many are teaching today about forgiveness.

■ *"I Will Forgive You If . . ."*

This tragic letter recently appeared in Ann Landers' column:

> Dear Ann Landers:
> Thank you for educating millions of people about incest. I am forty-two and still recovering from my nightmarish childhood. The molester was my father, and it started at age seven and continued until I was twelve.
> I was the victim of my parents' sado masochistic marriage. My father was a sex addict and an alcoholic. My mother was a codependent and a sex addict and an alcoholic enabler. In the eyes of the community, we were the perfect family. No one would have believed what went on behind those closed doors. The childhood sexual abuse caused me to have severe health problems as well as trouble with school, employment, and social relationships. I felt crazy and couldn't understand why. Strange as it seems, I never made the connection. . . . My father died in 1972 and I didn't shed a tear. His tombstone should say, "Child Molester." Thanks, Ann. Writing this letter has helped me to dissipate some of my anger.[1]

How can this woman ever hope to be released from the understandable rage and bitterness she feels over her abuse? Is it possible that she could ever forgive her parents? Unfortunately, many counselors (even Christian counselors) would tell her that she can only forgive her parents if they are willing to admit their guilt and make restitution for their offenses. Otherwise, to try to forgive an unrepentant offender places "an undue burden on the victim." Such counseling is known as "restitution therapy." The following material, written to incest victims, is typical of such therapy:

> Dear Victim:
>
> If you are like most victims who have been sexually abused, you are asking many questions of yourself.

We have all heard the old favorites from sex offenders, family members, ministers, and clergy, "Forgive and forget; let bygones be bygones; let's bury the hatchet and start over." These statements seem to encourage victims to feel as though it is their responsibility to take action regarding resolution and forgiveness. This seems strange since victims are innocent and not responsible for what has occurred. ...We believe you as a victim are innocent, and we demand restitution be paid to you in some form. You will learn that your rehabilitation is our goal. You are not responsible for the sexual abuse, and you are not responsible for forgiveness. Your sexual offender is responsible for both these things....[2]

Obviously, there are a number of serious flaws with this type of therapy. First, it assumes the total innocence of the victim—and no one is totally innocent. No, I am not suggesting that the 42-year-old incest victim was responsible for her father's attack when she was only seven. But I am saying that the woman has been guilty of *other* offenses throughout her life. And such a realization of one's own guilt is absolutely necessary before we can forgive others. Why? Remember Jesus' parable about the two debtors? Only when you understand the tremendous debt God has forgiven you will you be able to forgive others.

Secondly, restitution therapy misinterprets the scriptural teachings about forgiveness. Such therapists who happen to know something about the Bible love to cite Matthew 18:15-17 and Luke 17:3-4 as proof that the offender must repent before he can be forgiven. But a closer examination of those passages dispels that myth. Matthew 18:15-17 refers to church discipline. Yes, there are some preconditions necessary before an unrepentant Christian can be allowed back into the fellowship of the church. But when Peter changes the subject to personal offenses (vv. 21-22), Jesus gives no conditions for forgiveness. The command to forgive a person "seventy times seven" implies that the offender is unrepentant, since he continues to offend. Nevertheless, we are to forgive him.

In Luke 17:3-4 Jesus does command us to forgive those who sin against us continually and ask forgiveness. But nowhere does Jesus say, "If they do not repent, don't forgive them." Our forgiveness of others is to be patterned after God's forgiveness of us—total and unconditional.

Thirdly, restitution therapy binds us emotionally to the offender rather than freeing us. The word for "forgiveness" means "release"—we are to release people of their offenses against us. Yet, if we demand that the offender behave a certain way before we can forgive him, we are not released but emotionally chained to that person. What happens if the offender refuses to repent? Or, as in the case of the incest victim, what if the offender dies? Are we destined to a lifetime of anger and bitterness?

While restitution therapy may sound logical, and even biblical, it actually contradicts the biblical principles of forgiveness and, as a result, offers no lasting solutions. How *can* we forgive those who have hurt us? Fortunately, the Bible provides some clear steps to help us choose forgiveness over bitterness.

■ *Joseph: A Case Study in Forgiveness*

Family relationships provide great potential for bitterness! Consider the story of Joseph, the favorite son of Jacob. Joseph's other eleven brothers were bitter over his favorite son status, so they sold him into slavery. Through a series of miraculous circumstances, Joseph ended up in Egypt as Pharaoh's right-hand man. A severe famine caused the brothers to travel from Israel to Egypt in search of food. Little did they know that the man to whom they would make their appeal for food was their own brother Joseph.

Once Joseph revealed his identity to his brothers, they were understandably apprehensive. Would Joseph extract revenge for his mistreatment? Much to their surprise, Joseph spoke lovingly to them. He recounted the way that God had used their offense for his good, his brother's good, and indeed for the good of the future Israelite nation. Had Joseph not been in Pharaoh's court, the future nation of Israel might have starved to death! Joseph's attitude about his brothers' offense is best summed up in

Genesis 50:20: "And as for you, you meant evil against me, but God meant it for good in order to bring about this present result, to preserve many people alive."

Joseph's story reveals some necessary steps of action to forgive someone who has hurt us.

1. *Acknowledge you have been hurt.* The more I counsel, the more I am convinced that one of the most potent forces in the universe is the power of denial. "That really didn't happen to me" or "It really wasn't as bad as it seemed" or "If I will just stay busy, I won't have to think about it." Many times we confuse forgiveness with dismissal.

When I began writing this chapter, I commented to my wife, "You know, I have a lot of faults, but bitterness is not one of them. I am a very forgiving person, don't you think?" She gave me one of those looks that only a wife can give, and proceeded to remind me of a few events I had forgotten. What I soon realized was that I had confused forgiveness with denial. Just because I am able to emotionally and mentally dismiss an offense does not mean that I have forgiven the offense.

I recalled two people who had hurt me several years ago. I had distanced myself from those people and spent little time thinking about them. But whenever their name arose in conversation, I would have some cutting remark to make. I had not forgiven the offenses; I had merely buried them.

One reason we engage in denial is because often the experience is too painful to acknowledge, so we block it out. Another reason for denial is that sometimes an offense leads us to the wrong conclusion that something must be wrong with us. We become obsessed with our offender's motivation in hurting us. "What is so wrong with me that my spouse would desert me (or) my friend would betray me (or) my parents would abuse me?"

I think that Joseph was tempted to feel this way. When Joseph first confronted his brothers, he made all of the Egyptians leave the room (Gen. 45:1). Why? I doubt that Joseph had ever revealed to his servants how he came to Egypt. Such a story was much too embarrassing. What flaw caused his brothers to hate him so intensely?

Yet when the time came for Joseph to speak to his brothers, he did not try to minimize the sin they had committed against him. "You meant it for evil," he charged. Such a realization was necessary before Joseph could forgive his brothers.

Psychiatrists Frank Minirth and Paul Meier remind us that there are at least six categories of people who need our forgiveness: our parents, ourselves, God (we can feel angry toward or disappointed with God, even though He has done nothing wrong), our spouse, those in authority over us, and others in our lives. Possibly there are hurts in your life which you have denied. Examine these six categories and list any actions that you need to forgive:

Parents:

Yourself:

God:

Spouse:

Authority Figures:

Others:

2. *See your hurt from God's perspective.* Instead of asking, "Why did this person do this to me?" ask yourself, "What is God trying to accomplish through this event?" If we believe in the sovereignty of God, we have to believe that nothing happens to us apart from God's divine plan. Now I can hear some of you saying, "Wait just a minute! Are you trying to say that everything that happens to me is good?" No. Everything that happens is not good. But God

can take the worst things that happen to us and use them for His eternal purpose in our lives. That is what Romans 8:28 is all about: "And we know that God causes all things to work together for good to those who love God, to those who are called according to His purpose."

The key to understanding this verse is properly defining "good." Unfortunately, we have an extremely shallow understanding of "good." We define "good" in terms of instant understanding or short-term happiness. But God has a much larger perspective concerning what is good. In fact, Paul goes on to define the "good" that God is trying to accomplish in our lives: "For whom He foreknew, He also predestined to become conformed to the image of His Son, that He might be the first-born among many brethren" (Rom. 8:29). Simply put, God has one purpose in your life—to make you like His Son. Thus, all things that happen in your life—especially the hurtful things—are being used by God to mold you into the image of Christ.

Why "especially the hurtful things"? Look at Hebrews 5:8. "Although He [Jesus] was a Son, He learned obedience from the things which He suffered." I do not pretend to fully understand all the Christological ramifications of this verse. But I do understand that suffering enhanced Jesus' relationship with His Father. If God's plan for His Son included suffering, and if we are called to be like Christ, should it be any surprise that part of God's plan for our lives should include unjust suffering?

The reason we are not to become obsessed with our offender's motivation in hurting us is that it is really immaterial. God is able to take the worst offenses that are committed against us and use them for our good and for His eternal glory. That is why Joseph said to his brothers, "You meant it for evil, but God meant it for good in order to bring about this present result, to preserve many people alive."

There were both short-term and long-term benefits of the brothers' injustice against Joseph. By their treacherous act, Joseph ended up in Egypt, where he was able to save the lives of many Egyptians and his own family by interpreting Pharaoh's dream of the coming famine. Not only that, but Joseph's family was able to settle in the rich Egyptian land of Goshen, where they multiplied into the mighty nation of Israel. Four hundred years later that nation left Egypt and entered into the Promised Land. And it was from that nation that the Savior of the world was born! All of that was accomplished through just one injustice!

Recently, I counseled with a woman who suffered a miscarriage. She was disappointed in God. Although I could manufacture all kinds of benefits from this circumstance, I realized how hollow they would be. The truth is that there seemed to be little good in this situation. Sometimes God allows us to see a glimpse of His eternal purpose in the injustices of life; most times He doesn't. Yet the message of the Bible is that God *is* capable of using the most unfair circumstances of life to make us like Christ.

3. *Acknowledge your faults and receive God's forgiveness.* Have you ever noticed how difficult it is to write a check when you have no money in your account? It is even more difficult to try to forgive someone when you have not first been forgiven. Remember the model for forgiveness found in Ephesians 4:32? We are to forgive others "just as God in Christ also has forgiven [us]." How do you receive God's forgiveness?

First, it is important to identify offenses you have committed — against your family, against friends, against other Christians, or against God. Secondly, confess those offenses to God. And finally, receive God's forgiveness based on Christ's death for you. For a more detailed discussion on these steps, review the material in chapter 5, "Choosing Repentance over Guilt."

4. *Choose forgiveness over bitterness.* When we are offended, we have a clear choice to make. We can forgive the offender, or we can become bitter. Think what would have happened if Joseph had chosen an attitude of bitterness instead of forgiveness. He would have refused his brother's request for food; his family would have starved to death; the nucleus of the nation Israel would have withered; and theoretically, the promise of a Savior would have been unfulfilled, and you and I would be left to suffer the consequences of our sins.

Why choose forgiveness? Certainly, there is a relationship between our willingness to forgive and our eternal destiny. Jesus closed His parable about the two debtors with this application: "So shall My heavenly Father also do to you, if each of you does not forgive his brother from your heart" (Matt. 18:35). Notice how closely these words parallel Jesus' teaching in Matthew 6:14: "For if you forgive men for their transgressions, your heavenly Father will also forgive you. But if you do not forgive men, then your Father will not forgive your transgressions."

I do not believe Jesus is saying that forgiving others is a *requirement* for salvation but that it is the *result* of salvation. Our willingness to forgive others is evidence that God has forgiven us. Our inability to forgive others simply betrays the fact that we have never experienced forgiveness.

But there is also a relationship between our willingness to forgive and our quality of life today. Forgiveness leads to life; bitterness leads to emotional and sometimes physical death. Bitterness is a poison that not only defiles others, but also destroys us. The great theologian Frederick Buechner once wrote:

Of the Seven Deadly Sins, anger is possibly the most fun.
To lick your wounds, to smack your lips over grievances long past,
To roll over your tongue the prospect of bitter confrontation to come—
To savor the last toothsome morsel of both the pain you are giving and pain you are getting back.
In many ways it is a feast fit for a king.
The chief drawback is that what you are wolfing down is yourself.
The skeleton at the feast is you.

Are there hurts in your life which you have denied? Are there offenses which you have held on to? Acknowledge them, release them, and begin to experience the freedom that comes from choosing forgiveness over bitterness.

CHAPTER NINE

CHOOSING PRODUCTIVITY OVER LAZINESS

*"Poor is he who works with
a negligent hand, but the
hand of the diligent makes
rich."*   *Prov. 10:4*

■ My mother-in-law says she never knows what to get me for my birthday or Christmas, so she usually provides me with a gift certificate from one of my favorite stores. I intended to use last year's certificate, but I forgot it when I went shopping. Then when I was about to take it with me on a shopping trip, to my horror, I noticed that it had expired. I had surrendered an opportunity to exchange this piece of paper for something valuable—all because of my forgetfulness. Now, that gift certificate is lying on top of my dresser—a monument to my slothfulness!

Life is a lot like a gift certificate from God. We can spend our lives for things infinitely more valuable than department store merchandise; we can squander our lives away on trivial pursuits; or we can allow life to expire without exchanging it for anything. The choice is ours.

The premise of this book is that our lives are shaped by our attitudes—our responses to the circumstances of life. Since God has given each of us a specific measure of time, resources, and talents, we must choose how to respond to such gifts. We can choose to waste those gifts, or we can choose to maximize them. An attitude of laziness—or as the Bible calls it, slothfulness—results in squandering God's gifts. An attitude of productivity, however, results in a harnessing of those resources. In this chapter, we will examine the relationship between productivity and wealth, define slothfulness and its consequences, and discover some practical steps toward developing an attitude of productivity.

■ *Does the Bible Promise Riches?*

The Christian airwaves constantly bombard us with the televangelist's message promising riches to the faithful. Consider one preacher's "Seven Steps of Faith" (four of the steps will be sufficient for you to get the general idea!):

Step One: Let God Know What You Need from Him. New car. New job. Fitness. House. Finances. Salvation.

Step Two: Give God Your Best Gift.

Step Three: Pray the Prayer of Agreement. Take the prayer sheet I've enclosed and lay your hand on top of mine [photograph] and pray, "O God, I pray in agreement right now with my Brother, Bob. By faith we decree my miracle into existence in the name of Jesus. Father, I am giving my best gift to You today; therefore, we ask that You rebuke the devil from my life according to Malachi 3. Amen."

Step Four: Mail Your Prayer Request and Your Faith Gift Back to Me Today![1]

How to Write Your Own Ticket with God (Kenneth Hagin), *God's Will Is Prosperity* (Kenneth Copeland), and *How I Learned Jesus Was Not Poor* (Oral Roberts) are just a sampling of the mountain of books and booklets being consumed by believers searching for their sanctified pot of gold.

One of the problems with this heresy—a problem common among most heresies—is that there is just enough truth mixed with error to make it believable. The Bible *does* seem to promise prosperity to those who obey God's Word. Consider just some of the many verses in the Bible on this subject:

"Honor the Lord from your wealth, and from the first of all your produce: so your barns will be filled with plenty, and your vats will overflow with new wine" (Prov. 3:9-10).

"Poor is he who works with a negligent hand, but the hand of the diligent makes rich" (Prov. 10:4).

"It is the blessing of the Lord that makes rich, and He adds no sorrow to it" (Prov. 10:22).

"Adversity pursues sinners, but the righteous will be rewarded with prosperity" (Prov. 13:21).

"Much wealth is in the house of the righteous, but trouble is in the income of the wicked" (Prov. 15:6).

How are we to understand these verses? Some would argue that these verses were part of the old covenant between God and Israel—an agreement that rewarded obedience to God's commands with both spiritual and material blessings. However, the argument continues, the terms of this covenant are not applicable to Christians today.

Obviously, there are both commands and promises in the Old Testament that were peculiar to Israel. For example, Deuteronomy 28 contains this conditional promise:

Now it shall be, if you will diligently obey the Lord your God, being careful to do all His commandments which I command you today, the Lord your God will set you high above all the nations of the earth. And all these blessings shall come upon you and overtake you, if you will obey the Lord your God. . . . And the Lord will make you abound in prosperity, in the offspring of your body and in the offspring of your beast and in the produce of your ground, in the land which the Lord swore to your fathers to give you (vv. 1-2, 11).

God was clearly speaking to the nation Israel when He made that promise. To try to appropriate such a promise today would be a serious hermeneutical (interpretative) mistake. Yet are we then to conclude that *all* of the Old Testament is simply a record of God's dealings with Israel and that there is little or no application for Christians today? When Paul wrote that "all Scripture is inspired by God and is profitable," he was referring to the Old Testament (the New Testament had not yet been penned). Thus, to completely discount the Old Testament teachings about prosperity, simply because they fall in the first half of the Bible, would also be a serious mistake.

Others would argue that we should simply take the Old Testament teachings about prosperity at face value. The problem with that approach is reconciling such teachings with the New Testament. If, indeed, righteous living results in material prosperity, then what happened to Jesus, the Apostle Paul, and many of the first century Christians who were poverty-stricken? Consider this summary statement about the "prosperity" the early Christians enjoyed: "They were stoned, they were sawn in two, they were tempted, they were put to death with the sword; they went about in sheepskins, in goatskins; being destitute, afflicted, ill-treated" (Heb. 11:37).

Paul seemed to indicate that riches were the exception, not the norm, for the early church: "For consider your calling, brethren, that there were not many wise [called] according to the flesh, not many mighty, not many noble" (1 Cor. 1:26). A few months ago, when I was preaching on this passage in 1 Corinthians, I began the message by asking all of the millionaires in our congregation to stand. Guess what? No one stood. We have a congregation of about 800 in our church and no millionaires! That leads me to conclude that either God is displeased with every one of my members, or obedience to God does not always result in material blessings.

The point of this chapter is that while God has called *few* of us to a life of wealth, He has called *all* of us to a life of productivity. Being a Christian does not guarantee wealth, but following Christian principles about time, labor, and resources results in greater prosperity than ignoring those principles. Productivity is more than a series of activities (getting up earlier, managing our time better, investing our money more wisely, etc.). Such activities do contribute to a more productive life. But such activities are the result of a basic attitude toward life's resources. Productivity is an attitude that views those resources as gifts from God to be maximized to the fullest.

Productivity is better understood by looking at the biblical antonymn of this attitude—slothfulness.

■ *Let's Take a Field Trip*

The Book of Proverbs contains a wealth of information about slothfulness and its consequences. The person who squanders his God-given assets is referred to as "the sluggard" or sometimes, "the fool." Although Proverbs gives much detailed information about the characteristics of the sluggard, no passage in the Bible better illustrates the results of slothful living than Proverbs 24:30-34:

> I passed by the field of the sluggard, and by the vineyard of the man lacking sense; and behold, it was completely overgrown with thistles; its surface was covered with nettles, and its stone wall was broken down. When I saw, I reflected upon it; I looked, and received instruction. "A little sleep, a little slumber, a little folding of the hands to rest," then your poverty will come as a robber, and your want like an armed man.

As the writer of Proverbs was taking his morning stroll, he could not help but notice his neighbor's yard. The land was completely overgrown, the wall around the property had fallen down—the place was a complete wreck! Have you ever noticed how almost every neighborhood seems to have at least one of these homes? Our usual response to such a neighbor is anger. "He's ruining the neighborhood" or "How can I sell my property with a disaster area like that next door?"

But instead of becoming irritated at his neighbor's neglect, the writer of Proverbs chose to learn from it. "This property did not become this way by accident. There are attitudes and actions that led to this situation." This seeker of wisdom wanted to learn from his neighbor's mistakes. I like the way the *New International Version* renders verse

32: "I applied my heart to what I observed and learned a lesson from what I saw."

And what was the lesson to be learned? The writer repeats his observation from Proverbs 6:10 (NIV): "A little sleep, a little slumber, a little folding of the hands to rest, and poverty will come as a bandit." Obviously, the writer is not saying that sleep, rest, or relaxation is evil. This verse is best understood as the sluggard's stock reply whenever someone challenges him to get his act together: "Just let me rest a little while longer, and I'll get around to it." The writer says that "just a little more sleep" eventually leads to poverty. I like what Derek Kidner says about the sluggard:

The wise man will learn while there is time. He knows that the sluggard is no freak, but, as often as not, an ordinary man who has made too many excuses, too many refusals, and too many postponements. It has all been as imperceptible, and as pleasant, as falling asleep.[2]

The writer of Proverbs sprinkled his entire book with his observations about the sluggard. We would do well to "apply to [our] heart" those same lessons. How do you recognize a sluggard?

1. *The sluggard refuses to begin a job.* The sluggard's motto is "Never do today what can be done tomorrow." His life is characterized by procrastination and rationalization. Instead of loving work, the slothful person loves sleep. "Like the door turns on its hinges, so does the sluggard on his bed" (26:14). When the sluggard finally can stay in bed no longer, he formulates all kinds of excuses for not working. Note one of the sluggard's more imaginative excuses: "There is a lion in the road! A lion is in the open square!" (26:13)

Let's be honest. There is a little of sluggard in most of us. Remember those dreaded term papers in high school and college? Although you would be given the assignment months ahead of time, only the class nerd would begin working on the paper the first day! "Why sweat this paper?

I have months to do it!" But as the days quickly expired and the deadline loomed on the horizon, our lackadaisical attitude suddenly gave way to panic. And that panic paralyzed us so that we could not begin. Finally, the week—or, yes, I'll admit it—the *night* before the due date, we would feverishly churn out a less than satisfactory paper, despising ourselves with every word we wrote, and vowing *never* to do this again.

Never say "never." Many people have carried that pattern of work into their adult lives. Projects at work, in the home, or even in our spiritual lives are postponed until a more convenient time arrives. Unfortunately, such excuses presume upon the future. And God gives us no assurance that we will have tomorrow. James, the half-brother of Jesus, had a pointed admonition to those who would presume upon the future: "Come now, you who say, 'Today or tomorrow, we shall go to such and such a city, and spend a year there and engage in business and make a profit.' Yet you do not know what your life will be like tomorrow. You are just a vapor that appears for a little while and then vanishes away" (4:13-14).

2. *The sluggard does not complete his work.* In the rare event that the sluggard runs out of excuses and actually begins a job, he will not complete it satisfactorily. For example, look at Proverbs 12:27: "A slothful man does not roast his prey, but the precious possession of a man is diligence." The sluggard catches his prey, but he refuses to cook it and, as a result, it spoils. Proverbs 19:24 illustrates just how lazy the sluggard is: "The sluggard buries his hand in the dish, and will not even bring it back to his mouth." Again, he completes the first step in a task; he puts his hand in the bowl, but he will not finish the task.

Or, if he happens to "finish" the task, his work is mediocre, at best. John F. Kennedy once said, "Success hinges on a passion for excellence." The word *excellence* is not in the sluggard's vocabulary. When you confront the sluggard about his substandard work, he gets a quizzical look on his face. "What's wrong with it?" he whines. He really doesn't understand. As Joubert said, "Mediocrity is excellent to the eye of the mediocre."

My old accordian teacher used to say, "Remember, it only costs a little more to go first class." Just a few more minutes of practicing "Lady of Spain" spelled the difference between mediocrity and excellence. Someone has said that the difference between an amateur and a professional is about five minutes more.

> Just five minutes more of reading toward your goal.
> Just five minutes more of working out a communication problem with your spouse.
> Just five minutes more with a son or daughter who may be having difficulties in school.
> Just five minutes more of asking God to give you the special guidance you so desperately need.[3]

Motivational expert Og Mandino writes about the importance of persevering until the job is completed:

> I will never consider defeat and will remove from my vocabulary such words and phrases as quit, cannot, unable, impossible, out of the question, improbable, failure, unworkable, hopeless and retreat: for they are the words of fools. I will avoid despair, but if this disease of the mind should infect me, then I will work on in despair. I will toil and I will endure. I will ignore the obstacles at my feet and keep mine eyes on the goals above my head, for I know that where dry desert ends, green grass grows. . . . I will forget the happenings of the day that is gone, whether they were good or bad, and greet the new sun with confidence that this will be the best day of my life.[4]

3. *The sluggard ignores opportunities.* The problem with the sluggard in Proverbs 24 was not that he slept—everyone needs rest. But he slept at the wrong time. He should have been preparing his field for sowing seed. Instead, he allowed the land to become overgrown, so that he was unable to plant a crop. When harvest time arrived, the sluggard reaped the results of his laziness—poverty.

To the sluggard, opportunities are like trains—there'll be

another one along every five minutes. In truth, opportunities are quite rare and often out of our control. The sluggard does not take advantage of such opportunities because either he is not prepared to take advantage of them or the opportunities arrive disguised as hard work.

For example, how many times have you heard the lament "If only I had invested in XYZ stock ten years ago, I would be a millionaire today"? Most often, the reason that person did not invest in that opportunity is lack of preparation. Instead of saving his money for unexpected opportunities, the sluggard squanders it.

Or, have you ever heard someone say, "I had the same idea for that product years ago. Why didn't I do something about it?" The answer is quite simple. Such action necessitates hard work—effort the sluggard is unwilling to expend. Thus, the sluggard's lack of preparation and his unwillingness to work cause him to miss opportunities. The result is a continual refrain of "If only...."

4. *The sluggard craves riches.* Although the sluggard shuns work, he still wants to enjoy the rewards of work. Thus he must find some way other than work to achieve wealth. He is usually a sucker for any get-rich-quick scheme that comes along. But such schemes always end in disaster: "He who makes haste to be rich will not go unpunished" (Prov. 28:20).

Or the sluggard often talks about a "big deal" he is working on. The operative word there is "talk." His "work" consists of endless fantasizing. The writer of Proverbs described the result of such fantasies: "In all labor there is profit, but more talk leads only to poverty" (Prov. 14:23). "He who tills his land will have plenty of food, but he who follows empty pursuits will have poverty in plenty" (Prov. 28:19).

5. *The sluggard's bad habits extend into every area of his life.* I have never known a sluggard who was slothful in his work but diligent in his walk with God. A sluggard's slothfulness usually extends into every area of his life: his family, his finances, his physical appearance, his intellectual development, his spiritual life, and so on. Such was the case of English poet Samuel Taylor Coleridge. Although he

possessed great talent, he never was able to fully harness his abilities. He pursued a vain attempt to build a Utopian community in the United States, he was often guilty of plagiarism, and he was addicted to opium. William Barclay summarizes the slothfulness of Coleridge:

> Coleridge is the supreme tragedy of indiscipline. Never did so great a mind produce so little. He left Cambridge University to join the Army; he left the Army because he could not rub down a horse; he returned to Oxford and left without a degree. He began a paper called *The Watchman* which lived for ten numbers and then died. It has been said of him: "He lost himself to visions of work to be done, that always remained to be done. Coleridge has every poetic gift but one—the gift of sustained and concentrated effort."[5]

In summary, slothfulness is an attitude of indifference toward the time, talent, resources, and opportunities God gives us. Such an attitude results in poverty and dissatisfaction in this life and a loss of rewards in the next life (see Matt. 25:14-30).

■ *On the Road to Productivity*

Hopefully, our short visit to the sluggard's field had the same effect on you as it did on the writer of Proverbs. I believe that he left that overgrown vineyard with a renewed determination to uproot his own life of any slothful habits. What can you do to turn such a resolve into concrete actions? Here are five suggestions about how to develop productivity in your life:

1. *Clearly define your purpose, objectives, and goals in life.* As mentioned in chapter 2, purpose is the engine that drives our lives. Without a clearly defined purpose for living, one has little motivation to harness his God-given resources. Why should I get up early, work hard, sharpen my skills, and save my money, unless I have a clear reason for doing so? The most unproductive people I know are those who could never articulate their purpose, objectives, and goals in life. Their sloth is symptomatic of their lack of purpose.

I hope you acted on the suggestions in chapter 2 for formulating your life purpose and the specific goals that contribute to that purpose. One word of caution. Don't ever think you have "arrived." Complacency is the greatest enemy of productivity. When we accomplish one goal, we should replace it with another so that we are always striving for something. Why? As Cervantes said, "The journey is better than the end."

2. *Manage your time effectively.* The most productive people are those who treasure every minute of life as a gift from God. They do not measure time by the decades, years, or even months, but by the hours, minutes, and seconds. They are constantly asking themselves the question, "What is the most productive thing I could be doing *now?*"

Valuing time is a biblical concept. Moses reminded us of the brevity of life. Seventy years, normally—eighty years perhaps. In light of the brevity of life, he prayed, "So teach us to number our days, that we may present to Thee a heart of wisdom" (Ps. 90:12). James echoed the same idea when he reminds us that our life is like a mist that appears for just a moment and then vanishes (James 4:14).

A myriad of books are available on the subject of time management. The following story suggests the advice given in these books:

When Charles Schwab was president of Bethlehem Steel Company, he asked well-known consultant Ivy Lee to help him become more productive. "Show me a way to get more things done with my time, and I will pay you any fee within reason." Lee gave Schwab a piece of paper and said, "Write down the most important tasks you have to do tomorrow and number them in order of importance. When you arrive in the morning, begin at once on No. 1 and stay on it till it's completed. Recheck your priorities; then begin with No. 2. If any task takes all day, never mind. Stick with it as long as it's the most important one. If you don't finish them all, you probably couldn't do so with any other method, and without some system you'd probably not even decide which one was most important. Make this a habit every working day. When it works for you, give it to your men. Try it as long as you like. Then send me your check for what you think it's worth."

A few weeks later, Lee received a check for $25,000 and a note from Schwab saying this was the most valuable advice he had ever received. Five years later, Bethlehem Steel Corporation was the largest independent steel producer in the world. Schwab said that the $25,000 fee he paid Lee was the most valuable investment Bethlehem Steel had ever made.[6]

Before you go to bed at night, take a moment and jot down the six most important things you can accomplish the next day. The next day, you will have a plan of action that will focus your energies on the most important tasks. Like Lee advised, don't be discouraged if you don't complete the list. At least you will have concentrated your efforts on your highest priorities.

3. *Make your financial resources according to God's plans.* Slothfulness and poverty go hand in hand. The sluggard's poverty is not only a result of his unwillingness to work, but is also a result of his failure to follow God's wisdom about money. Ignoring biblical teachings about money results in financial bondage. And such bondage is a hindrance to achieving one's life purpose. People who are constantly worried about paying this week's rent are rarely concerned about long-term goals and objectives. Instead, as Thoreau said, they are sentenced to living lives of quiet desperation.

John D. Morgan, a Houston pastor, gives some symptoms of financial bondage:

1. When you charge daily expenditures because of a lack of funds.

2. When you put off paying a bill until next month.

3. When you borrow to pay fixed expenses such as taxes or insurance.

4. When you have creditors calling or writing about past due bills.

5. When you take money from savings to pay current bills.

6. When you have less than three months' ex-

penses in an available account for emergencies.

7. When you find returning your tithe to God difficult.[7]

As mentioned at the beginning of this chapter, God has called few Christians to wealth, but He has called all of us to productivity. The goal of the biblical teachings about money is not to make us wealthy but to make us free to achieve our life purpose. Like the subject of time management, there are bookshelves full of books on the subject of Christian financial management. The Book of Proverbs gives advice on financial management that will save you from financial bondage:

● *Avoid debt.* Proverbs 22:7 warns, "The borrower becomes the lender's slave." The problem with debt is that it presumes about the future. And a Christian should never do that. "Do not boast about tomorrow, for you do not know what a day may bring forth" (Prov. 27:1). To borrow money with no certain way of repaying is foolish. Debt may be necessary for some larger items like a home or an automobile. But even in those circumstances, first ask yourself this question: "If disaster struck, would I be able to repay that debt without going into bankruptcy?" Sometimes the residual value of the item would protect you in case of default. In most cases, however, the gap between the resale value of the item and the debt could spell trouble.

● *Beware of cosigning for someone else's debt.* The only thing more foolish than presuming upon your future is presuming on someone else's! Proverbs 17:18 reminds us that "a man lacking in sense pledges and becomes surety in the presence of his neighbor."

● *Save some of your earnings systematically.* The sluggard has no reserve funds. When times are good, he spends everything he earns. But he fails to plan for the future. The writer of Proverbs had this advice for the sluggard: "Go to the ant, O sluggard, observe her ways and be wise, which, having no chief officer or ruler, prepares her food in the summer, and gathers her provision in the harvest" (6:6-8). Financial experts generally agree that we should save at least 10 percent of our income every month.

In addition to that, in case of a loss of income or disaster, every person should have a reserve fund of three to six months' living expenses.

● *Do not be entrapped by greed.* The sluggard's greed is usually his downfall. His desire for wealth without work is so strong that he is susceptible to foolish and sometimes illegal schemes. Proverbs 11:6 says that "the treacherous will be caught by their own greed." Greed not only impairs our judgment, but it also causes us to forfeit what is most important in life. Remember Paul's words to Timothy on this subject? "But those who want to get rich fall into temptation and a snare and many foolish and harmful desires which plunge men into ruin and destruction. For the love of money is a root of all sorts of evil, and some by longing for it have wandered away from the faith, and pierced themselves with many a pang" (1 Tim. 6:9-10).

Survey highly productive people, and you will find that most of them respect money; but they do not reverence it. They do what they do not for money but because of a burning passion to achieve. The accomplished violinist, the prolific author, the champion athlete will all tell you that money is a nice by-product of their efforts. But they will also tell you that if they ever begin focusing their attention on money, they will become distracted and hindered from achieving their goals.

4. *Discipline yourself for a productive life.* Let's admit it. Most of us are basically lazy. Given a choice, we will usually take the easy way out. Such a realization is necessary if we are going to achieve our life purpose. Just like the Apostle Paul, we too must continually work to master our bodies (see 1 Cor. 9:27).

Maybe you have a burning desire to live a productive life, but your life is in such disarray you do not know where to begin. Furthermore, you doubt you have the self-discipline to pull it off anyway. Where should you begin? Several years ago, John MacArthur wrote some practical suggestions for getting out of the rut of slothfulness:

● Start small. Start with your room. Clean it, then keep it clean. When something is out of place, train yourself to put it where it belongs. Then extend that discipline of neatness to the rest of your home.

● Be on time. That may not sound very spiritual, but it's important. If you're supposed to be somewhere at a specific time, be there on time! Develop the ability to discipline your desires, activities, and demands so that you can arrive on time.

● Do the hardest job first. Doing that will prevent the hardest jobs from being left undone.

● Organize your life. Plan the use of your time; don't just react to circumstances. Use a calendar and make a daily list of things you need to accomplish. If you don't control your time, everything else will!

● Accept correction. Correction helps make you more disciplined because it shows you what you need to avoid. Don't avoid criticism; accept it gladly.

● Practice self-denial. Learn to say no to your feelings. Occasionally deny yourself things that are all right just for the purpose of mastering yourself. Learn to do what you know to be right even if you don't feel like doing it. Cultivating discipline in the physical realm will help us become disciplined in our spiritual lives.

● Welcome responsibility. When you have an opportunity to do something that needs to be done, volunteer for it if you have talent in that area. Welcoming responsibility forces you to organize yourself.[8]

5. *Define "productivity" correctly.* Make sure you are focusing your time, talents, and resources on that which is really important in life. In his book *When All You've Ever Wanted Is Not Enough,* Harold Kushner makes an interesting observation:

Ask the average person which is more important to him, making money or being devoted to his family, and virtually everyone will answer family without hesitation. But watch how the average person actually lives out his life. See where he really invests his time and energy, and he will give away the fact that he does not really live by what he says he believes. He has let himself be persuaded that if he leaves for work earlier in the morning and comes home more tired at night, he is proving how devoted he is to his family by expending himself to provide them with all the things they have seen advertised. Ask the average person which means more to her, the approval of strangers or the affection of people closest to her, and she won't be able to understand why you would even ask such a question. Obviously, nothing means more to her than her family and her closest friends. Yet how many of us have embarrassed our children or squelched their spontaneity, for fear of what neighbors or strangers might think? How often have we poured out our anger on those closest to us because we had a hard day at work or someone else did something to upset us? And how many of us have let ourselves become irritable with our families because we were dieting to make ourselves look more attractive to people who do not know us well enough to see beyond appearances?[9]

Let me add to the author's observations. Ask the average Christian to prioritize the following objectives in life: making money, being successful in business, spending time with family and friends, and serving God, and most will rank "serving God" at the top of the list. Yet, our actions betray our words. Our relationship with God is usually the recipient of our leftover time, money, and abilities.

To have a truly productive life, we must expend our efforts in those areas which will have the greatest return. And since the Bible teaches that everything on this earth will be consumed by fire, doesn't it make sense to spend our lives on that which will last for eternity? Jesus put it this way, "For what will a man be profited, if he gains the whole world, and forfeits his soul?" (Matt. 16:26).

CHAPTER TEN

CHOOSING HUMILITY OVER PRIDE

"For who regards you as superior? And what do you have that you did not receive? But if you did receive it, why do you boast as if you had not received it?"   *1 Cor. 4:7*

■ Senator Bill Bradley of New Jersey tells the story of a humbling visit to a restaurant. The waiter brought over the rolls, but no butter.

"May I have some butter, please?" Bradley asked.

The waiter gave a slight nod and wandered off, but ten minutes later, no butter. Bradley caught the waiter's eye.

"May I please have some butter?"

The waiter barely acknowledged the request. After ten more minutes, still no butter.

"Maybe you don't know who I am," said Bradley. "I'm a Princeton graduate, a Rhodes scholar, and an All-American basketball player who played with the New York Knicks in the pros. I'm currently a United States senator from New Jersey, chairman of the International Debt Subcommittee of the Senate Finance Committee, chairman of the Water and Power Subcommittee of the Senate Energy and Natural Resources Committee, and a member of the Senate Select Intelligence Committee."

"Maybe you don't know who I am," said the waiter. "I'm the guy who's in charge of the butter."

What happened after that isn't known, but occasionally we all need to have someone burst our balloon of self-importance and bring us back to reality. Such experiences are healthy because they help us maintain a proper perspective about our accomplishments. Pride is an attitude that causes us to credit ourselves for our accomplishments and to blame others for our failures. On the other hand, humility is an attitude that views both our accomplishments and our failures from God's perspective.

In this book, we have learned that attitudes are our emotional and mental responses to the circumstances in life. How do you react to the inevitable successes and failures in your life? In this chapter, we will examine the biblical foundation and some practical suggestions for choosing humility over pride.

■ *Pride vs. Humility*

A brief examination of Scripture reveals God's attitude toward pride and humility. Notice some of the Bible's numerous condemnations of a prideful attitude:

"Everyone who is proud in heart is an abomination to the Lord; assuredly, he will not be unpunished" (Prov. 16:5).
"Pride goes before destruction, and a haughty spirit before stumbling" (Prov. 16:18).
"Haughty eyes and a proud heart, the lamp of the wicked, is sin" (Prov. 21:4).
"God is opposed to the proud, but gives grace to the humble" (James 4:6).

In contrast, notice how the attitude of humility is exalted:

"When pride comes, then comes dishonor, but with the humble is wisdom" (Prov. 11:2).
"It is better to be of a humble spirit with the lowly, than to divide the spoil with the proud" (Prov. 16:19).

"But to this one I will look, to him who is humble and contrite of spirit, and who trembles at My word" (Isa. 66:2).

"And whoever exalts himself shall be humbled, and whoever humbles himself shall be exalted" (Matt. 23:12).

"All of you, clothe yourselves with humility toward one another, for God is opposed to the proud, but gives grace to the humble. Humble yourselves, therefore, under the mighty hand of God, that He may exalt you at the proper time" (1 Pet. 5:5-6).

■ *The Problem with Pride*

Why does God hate pride so much? Why is pride at the top of the list of the seven deadly sins mentioned in Proverbs 6? Remember the definition of pride? It is the attitude that credits ourselves with our successes and blames others for our failures. Such an attitude is the root cause of the following sins:

● *Ingratitude.* My two-year-old daughter was at the stage where she was very conscious of who had given her what gift. She labeled all of her clothes and toys according to who gave the gift. One day she held up a gift and said "Grandma." But she was mistaken. Grandma had not given her the gift — I had! Yes, I'll admit it sounds silly, but I was perturbed because she was crediting someone else with my gift. I wanted my daughter to know I had given her the gift. Why? Because I wanted her to perceive the gift as a demonstration of my love for her.

Pride prevents us from crediting God with the good things in our lives. Instead, we reach the erroneous conclusion that whatever we value in our lives — our appearance, our abilities, our families, our possessions — are somehow the result of our effort. Such a conclusion is understandable. We live in a culture that worships individualism and self-effort. "I am the captain of my fate; I am the master of my soul." Our history is filled with Horatio Alger stories — rags to riches. Many of our ancestors came to Ellis Island with only a cardboard suitcase and a dogged determination to succeed. And they did just that! Such inspiring stories lead to the worship of the human spirit: "Anything the mind can conceive and believe, it can achieve."

But wait a minute! Before we get too caught up in our own importance, we need again to consider the Apostle Paul's sobering question to bring us back to reality: "For who regards you as superior? And what do you have that you did not receive? But if you did receive it, why do you boast as if you had not received it?" (1 Cor. 4:7).

Think about it for a moment, Paul advises. What good thing in your life is not ultimately a gift from God?

Your appearance? "I work out every day and watch my diet. I subscribe to *Vogue*. That's why I'm so attractive." While it is possible to enhance or neglect your appearance, God's Word reminds us that every part of our body was formed in our mother's womb before we were born: "For thou didst form my inward parts; thou didst weave me in my mother's womb. I will give thanks to Thee, for I am fearfully and wonderfully made" (Ps. 139:13-14).

Your abilities? "My gift of _____ is the result of years of practice." Yes, we can capitalize on or squander the talents God has given us. But James 1:17 reminds us that "every good thing bestowed and every perfect gift is from above, coming down from the Father of lights, with whom there is no variation, or shifting shadow."

Your children? "My children are the result of biology and genetics!" (Translation: "They wouldn't be so great, if I wasn't so great.") Yet one only has to stand in a delivery room and witness the miracle of birth to realize the truth of Psalm 127:3: "Behold, children are a gift of the Lord; the fruit of the womb is a reward."

Your possessions? "I've worked hard all of my life. That's why I have what I have." In the last chapter, we saw the relationship between productivity and prosperity. Yet ultimately it is God who controls our financial destiny. Job's life was a living illustration of this truth. After suffering catastrophic losses, Job was reminded that God "shows no partiality to princes nor regards the rich above the poor, for they all are the work of His hands" (Job 34:19).

Simple logic leads you to the conclusion that *every* good

thing in life, beginning with the breath of life itself, is ultimately a gift from God. And yet pride blinds us to such an obvious truth.

● *Independence.* Is God so petty that He has to be given credit for everything or He pouts and sulks? Is God so insecure that He must have our undivided allegiance in life? While pettiness and insecurity may be my motivations in desiring my daughter's gratitude, they are not God's. Although God desires our fellowship, He doesn't need it. In human terminology, God is completely self-sufficient. He existed before His creation.

Why then the demand for our gratitude? God's desire for our allegiance is based on His love for us. God knows that it is impossible for us to be fulfilled apart from a relationship with Him. He made us that way – in His image. Unlike the animals, we are spirit beings. And that spiritual component of our lives can be satisfied only by God. "As Augustine wrote in the *City of God,* "There is a God-shaped vacuum in every man that only Christ can fill."

Think about it for a moment. If you were a loving God and wanted to get the attention of your creation, how would you do it? The same way a father tries to get the attention of his children – by giving them good gifts. Jesus pointed out this truth in Matthew 7:11: "If you then, being evil, know how to give good gifts to your children, how much more shall your Father who is in heaven give what is good to those who ask Him!" God's plan is to shower us with good gifts, so that we might desire to know the loving giver of those gifts.

Unfortunately, ingratitude – the result of pride – leads to independence. When we delude ourselves into thinking that we are somehow responsible for the good things in our lives, we decide we really don't need God. Such a false conclusion was the basis for Lucifer's fall from heaven. Look at God's explanation for Satan's downfall, recorded in the Book of Ezekiel: "You were blameless in your ways from the day you were created, until unrighteousness was found in you . . . Your heart was lifted up because of your beauty; you corrupted your wisdom by reason of your splendor" (28:15, 17).

Look closely at what God said. "Lucifer, you forgot that you are a creature, not the Creator. You failed to credit Me for your beauty and splendor. And because of that, pride has entered your heart." And what was the by-product of pride and ingratitude? A desire to operate independently from God. We find a record of Lucifer's "declaration of independence" in the Book of Isaiah: "But you said in your heart, 'I will ascend to heaven; I will raise my throne above the stars of God, and I will sit on the mount of assembly in the recesses of the north. I will ascend above the heights of the clouds; I will make myself like the Most High' " (14:13-14).

Independence—the belief that we are sufficient apart from God—is a deadly result of pride.

● *Intolerance.* As you examine the Gospels, you will see that Jesus did not deal harshly with adulterers, thieves, or even murderers. Jesus' harshest words were reserved for the self-righteous Pharisees. Their self-righteousness led to a hatred for other people and the false assumption that they were the only ones going to heaven. Jesus warned, "Woe to you, scribe, and Pharisees, hypocrites, because you shut off the kingdom of heaven from men; for you do not enter in yourselves, nor do you allow those who are entering to go in" (Matt. 23:13). Such intolerance of others is a direct result of pride. Jesus drew this connection between pride and intolerance in one of His parables:

And He also told this parable to certain ones who trusted in themselves that they were righteous, and viewed others with contempt: "Two men went up into the temple to pray, one a Pharisee, and the other a tax-gatherer. The Pharisee stood and was praying thus to himself, 'God, I thank Thee that I am not like the other people: swindlers, unjust, adulterers, or even like this tax-gatherer. I fast twice a week; I pay tithes of all that I get.' But the tax-gatherer, standing some distance away, was even unwilling to lift up his eyes to heaven, but was beating his breast, saying, 'God be merciful to me, the sinner!' I tell you, this man went down to his house justified rather than the other; for everyone who exalts himself shall be humbled, but he who humbles himself shall be exalted" (Luke 18:9-17).

An inflated view of ourselves leads to a disdain for others. Of course, we need to be on the alert. Pride is so subtle that we can become proud of our humility. We need to be careful that we are not like the Sunday School teacher who, after telling the story about the Pharisee and the tax-gatherer, said, "Children, let's bow our heads and thank the Lord that we are not like the Pharisee."

● *Inability to accept God's grace.* Perhaps the most tragic result of pride is the inability to accept God's forgiveness. If there is one sin that keeps a person out of heaven, it is pride. Jesus illustrated this truth in His story about the rich young ruler:

> And a certain ruler questioned Him, saying, "Good Teacher, what shall I do to inherit eternal life?" And Jesus said to him, "Why do you call Me good? No one is good except God alone. You know the commandments, 'Do not commit adultery, Do not murder, Do not steal, Do not bear false witness, Honor your father and mother.' " And he said, "All these things I have kept from my youth." And when Jesus heard this, He said to him, "One thing you still lack; sell all that you possess, and distribute it to the poor, and you shall have treasure in heaven; and come, follow Me." But when he had heard these things, he became very sad; for he was extremely rich (Luke 18:18-23).

A superficial reading of this story leads many to the false conclusion that money keeps people out of heaven or that one can buy his way into heaven by giving to the poor. But the young ruler's unwillingness to sell all he had was only symptomatic of a much deeper sin problem—a problem he had difficulty comprehending because of his pride.

Notice the self-righteous attitude of the young ruler. After being reminded of God's holiness, the ruler quickly replied that he had kept *all* of God's Law.

What an amazing statement! It is impossible for most of us to keep God's Law for an hour, much less an entire lifetime! When Jesus replied, "One thing you still lack," I believe He was speaking tongue-in-cheek. The Lord knew that this young man lacked *many* things. Jesus' request that he divest himself of his wealth was an attempt to demonstrate the young ruler's basic unrighteousness.

In the verse preceding this story, Jesus said, "Truly I say to you, whoever does not receive the kingdom of God like a child shall not enter it at all" (Luke 18:17). In our church, we frequently have children respond to the Gospel. Sometimes parents are reluctant to allow their children to make such a decision. "Don't they need to be older?" they often ask. Our mind-set is that children need to be like adults before they can become Christians. But Jesus says just the opposite—adults need to become like children before they can be saved! You see, a child usually has no problem admitting that he is a sinner and needs the Savior. Unlike the rich young ruler, children rarely are infected with such a severe case of self-righteousness that they are unable to accept the Gospel. That may explain why the average age of Christian converts is twelve, and there are so few adults who ever respond to the Gospel. Pride bars us from admitting our need for grace.

■ *Humility, not Humiliation*

I love the story about the snake that went to the optometrist for a pair of glasses.

"You can't wear glasses," said the optometrist. "You don't have a nose or ears on which to hang them. And besides, your eyes are in the wrong place. Let's try some contact lenses."

"All right," the snake agreed.

Several weeks later, the snake returned to the doctor.

"Have you been able to see better?" the doctor inquired.

"Yes, I can see fine. But I'm extremely depressed," the snake complained.

"Why is that?"

"I've just discovered that I have been living with a water hose all of these years!"

Clear vision can be painful! Humility is seeing ourselves—both our accomplishments and our failures—from
God's point of view. And such a shift in perspective is not
always pleasant! We have already seen that humility is necessary to receive God's grace. But besides helping us gain
entrance into heaven, humility also allows us to enjoy
healthy relationships with others.

What exactly is humility and how is it developed? Here
are five characteristics of humility:

1. *Humility is willing to credit others for our successes.* In his book *The Fine Art of Mentoring*, Ted Engstrom
recounts this story from Bernie May, director of Wycliffe
Bible Translators, about May's predecessor, "Uncle Cam"
Townsend:

> Several years after I moved to Peru I was elected
> chairman of the Executive Committee—which was the
> equivalent of being senior deacon in a church. Uncle
> Cam, who was general director of Wycliffe World-
> wide, came to me one hot, muggy afternoon. I had
> just come in from a long jungle flight in a single-
> engine float plane. I had flown out the night before,
> landed on the Maranon River and gotten up early the
> next morning to load two translators and their baby
> into the plane. They had an Indian language helper
> with them—plus a small cage with two monkeys and
> assorted baggage. It was a three-hour flight back and
> Uncle Cam was waiting for me when I landed.
>
> "Bernie," he began, "what do you think about invit-
> ing the Minister of Education out to the center for a
> reception?"
>
> "It sounds like a grand idea to me," I said. "We need
> to have more contact with the government officials."
>
> The following day I was attending a meeting of the
> Executive Committee when I heard Uncle Cam say,
> "Bernie thinks we ought to invite the Minister of Edu-
> cation to come out from Lima to attend an anniversa-
> ry reception at the center. I agree with him."
>
> Everyone else agreed too—and suddenly I was in
> the middle of all the details.

Uncle Cam was constantly giving credit to others — and to God. "Isn't it wonderful," he told a group of us one time, "how God has laid it on the heart of the President of Mexico to open the doors to enlarged ministry in the nation." We all agreed. It wasn't until much later that I learned that God had a lot of help from Uncle Cam who had spent days sitting in the waiting room outside El Presidente's office until the President finally capitulated and gave him an audience.[1]

The truly humble person is so consumed with his job as a servant that he is not concerned with who gets the credit for his work. Some years ago when my wife and I were in Washington, D.C., a friend of a friend who was a Secret Service agent took us on a late-night tour of the White House. We stood in one of the hallways and listened to the agent's walkie-talkie report that President Reagan was in the family quarters and preparing for bed. We then knew it was safe to enter the Oval Office. I will never forget one of the plaques on the President's desk. It read, "There is no limit to the good a person can do if he is willing to let someone else take the credit." I often thought of that plaque when I heard people recount the great successes of the Reagan presidency. Possibly it was that attitude that led many to characterize Reagan as one of this century's greatest presidents.

2. *Humility generates a genuine interest in others.* A humble person seeks to serve other people instead of using them. Such a person has adopted Jesus' mission statement: "The Son of Man did not come to be served, but to serve" (Matt. 20:28). Such a view of others is completely contrary to a culture which is characterized by books like *Winning through Intimidation* and *Looking Out for Number One*. Yet Jesus made it clear that "whoever wishes to become great among you shall be your servant" (Matt. 20:26).

Every year I travel to our denomination's annual convention and return with a resolve never to go again. I am constantly encountering egotistical preachers who are trying to climb over one another on their way up the success ladder. I think of one in particular. This pastor is consumed with the desire to be number one. He is interested in you only if you can help him achieve his goal. When you talk with him, he will never look you in the eye. Instead, his eyes are constantly darting around the room seemingly checking to see if there is anyone more important than you with whom he should be conversing. He is very careful that he is always in a group of people. If he is left alone for a minute, he becomes agitated and quickly tries to find a group to absorb him.

I compare him to two truly great Christian leaders I have met: Cliff Barrows, Billy Graham's longtime songleader, and Charles Stanley, widely known TV preacher and author. If you have ever conversed with either of these men, you know what I am talking about. They look you straight in the eye and give you their undivided attention, as if you were the only person in the room. The President of the United States could walk into the room, and neither man would take his eyes off you. The few times I have spoken with these men, I was amazed at the genuine interest they showed in me. They asked me questions about my family and my ministry. This was not a mere public relations ploy. I had nothing to offer them. They are genuinely interested in other people. Any success that has come their way is viewed as a result of God's grace and a vehicle for serving God and others. That is a mark of humility!

3. *Humility resists the need to always be right.* Popular speaker and author Chuck Swindoll tells the story about a Scandinavian couple named Sven and Holda. Both were Christians. He taught Sunday School; she sang in the choir. They had a family altar and family prayers. They went to church twice on Sundays and attended the midweek services, but they could not get along. They fought all the time. They felt guilty about their stormy relationship, and they prayed about it often. One morning after their quiet time with God, and yet still not getting along with one another, Holda said, "Sven, I think I've got the answer to this hopeless problem we have."

"Tell me, Holda, what is it?"

"I think we should pray for the Lord to take one of us to be home with Him. Then I can go and live with my sister."

Talk about pride! While a prideful attitude blames others for our failures, humility recognizes that the problem may be us. A humble person realizes that he does not have a monopoly on the truth. He is willing to admit that the other person might be right, at least on some points.

When you are in a disagreement with another person—a spouse, a child, a friend, a coworker, a church member—are you willing to admit that you may not be right? Do you really listen to that person, or are you so busy formulating your next statement that you don't hear what that person is trying to communicate? A humble person is willing to admit he is wrong.

An aging old preacher told a group of young ministers, "Men, I have eaten crow every way you can imagine—broiled, fried, baked, and roasted. And no matter how you prepare it, it never tastes good." Crow is a regular item on the menu of the humble!

4. *Humility views life's accomplishments and failures from God's perspective.* We Christians often have a difficult time maintaining a balanced view of ourselves. We usually gravitate to one of two extremes: "I am so wonderful, how could God ever get along without me?" to "I am just a lowly worm who can't do anything." Fortunately, the Bible does not substantiate either of those perspectives.

To the person who revels in his accomplishments, the Word of God has this reminder: "For through the grace given to me I say to every man among you not to think more highly of himself than he ought to think; but to think so as to have sound judgment, as God has allotted to each a measure of faith" (Rom. 12:3). Paul then goes on to discuss the truth of spiritual gifts: God has gifted each of us differently so that we might serve Him. Just as a body has many necessary parts for its smooth functioning, so the body of Christ is not one part, but many. No Christian was designed to function in isolation. We need one another.

To the person who is constantly berating himself as an under serving wretch, the Word of God has this reminder:

"Therefore if any man is in Christ, he is a new creature; the old things passed away; behold, new things have come" (2 Cor. 5:17). Yes, Jesus made it clear when He said that "apart from Me you can do nothing." But a Christian by definition is not apart from Christ. The doctrine of the baptism by the Holy Spirit teaches that when we become Christians we are totally immersed by God's Spirit so that "it is no longer I who live, but Christ lives in me" (Gal. 2:20).

Humility gives us God's perspective about ourselves— apart from Christ we are deserving of nothing but eternal punishment. But in Christ, we are capable of anything. Like the Apostle Paul, we can say, "I can do all things through Christ who strengthens me" (Phil. 4:13).

The story is told about the great conductor Toscanini as he was directing the New York Philharmonic in Beethoven's Ninth Symphony. Carnegie Hall was packed to capacity to hear the great conductor for the last time. The orchestra played like they had never played. At the end, the orchestra members rose to their feet in mad applause in honor of the conductor. He kept beating his baton against the stand to get their attention, but it was to no avail. Finally, after fifteen full minutes, he got their attention and said, "Gentlemen, it's not me, but Beethoven." That is the attitude of the humble Christian toward life's accomplishments—"It is not me, but Christ in me."

CHAPTER ELEVEN

CHOOSING COMPANIONSHIP OVER LONELINESS

"Two are better than one because they have a good return for their labor. For if either of them falls, the one will lift up his companion. But woe to the one who falls when there is not another to lift him up."
Eccl. 4:9-10

■ "Alone Again, Naturally," a popular song of several decades ago, is still heard on the radio. This depressing ballad recounts the sorrow of a young man who loses all of those close to him through either defection or death and concludes with the young man contemplating suicide. The refrain of each verse summarizes his plight — "alone again, naturally."

Unfortunately, loneliness does seem to be the norm for most people. Billy Graham claims that more people suffer from loneliness than from any other problem. Author Paul Tournier calls loneliness the most devastating problem of our time. Admiral Richard Byrd, the first man to fly over the North Pole, wrote in his diary at one point: "This morning I had to admit to myself that I was lonely. Try as I may, I can't take my loneliness casually. It is too big. I must not dwell on it; otherwise I am undone."[1]

Psychologists tell us that there are two types of loneliness. First, there is a loneliness that is the result of isolation of space. It is the sensation we feel when we are separated by distance from a loved one or familiar surroundings. But the second type of loneliness is far more severe. It is a loneliness of spirit.[2] It is the feeling of isolation that can be felt in a crowded room, in a church, or even in a marriage. Frederick Robertson wrote of this type of loneliness:

> There are times when hands touch ours, but only send an icy chill of unsympathizing indifference to the heart: when eyes gaze into ours, but with a glazed look which cannot read into the bottom of our souls—when words pass from our lips, but only come back as an echo reverberated without replying through a dreary solitude—when the multitude throng and press us, and we cannot say, as Christ said, "Somebody touched me," for the only contact has been not between soul and soul, but only between form and form.[3]

When we think of loneliness, we usually think of it as a state of being: either isolation of distance or spirit. But I believe that loneliness is more than a condition. It is a condition that often is the result of a basic attitude choice that says, "I am self-sufficient and can face life alone." If attitudes are responses to life circumstances, how do you choose to react to the joys and sorrows of life? You can choose to stoically face life alone, or you can choose an attitude of companionship—an attitude that says, "I need other people for my emotional and spiritual health."

■ *Why Would Anyone Choose to Be Lonely?*
Consider this sad story. I know of an elderly widower who discovered that he had cancer. After consulting with his physicians, he decided to travel to a distant state for an operation. The operation could have been fatal or have left him an invalid. Yet he never told any of his friends that he was facing serious surgery, or that he was even ill. Instead, he simply said that he was going on a trip. He packed his

belongings, closed up his house, and said good-bye to his friends, knowing that he might never return. When questioned about his refusal to tell his friends, he said, "I don't want to bother them with my problems."

I doubt that was the real reason. Why would anyone deliberately choose to face the crises of life alone? Here are six reasons that people choose to be lonely:

1. *Poor self-image.* Low self-esteem leads some people to ask, "Why would anyone be interested in me? I am not attractive, talented, or extroverted. I don't have enough education, money, or status to cause people to care about me." The person who cannot accept himself has a difficult time believing anyone else will either. Such a person is deeply fearful of rejection. "What if I reach out to this person, and I am rejected?" This individual's poor self-image simply cannot tolerate anymore rejection.

Let's face it. None of us likes rejection. No matter who we are, we all can remember times when we have been rebuffed by others: on the school playground when we were the last to be chosen for a team; by a special boyfriend or girlfriend in high school; by a fraternity or sorority in college; by a group of couples with whom we would like to socialize. Rejection is painful—but it is an occupational hazard of companionship. Think for a moment about people you have reached out to who *have* responded positively to your overtures: a co-worker, a church member, your best friend, your spouse. Most likely that relationship would not have materialized had you not taken some risks.

My father was an extremely intelligent, articulate, and witty person. He was a college graduate who held an important position with a large, international airline. But he was plagued by a poor self-image rooted in his childhood. His parents' bitter divorce and rancorous custody battles filled him with doubts about his own self-worth. As a result, he had no intimate friends, only acquaintances. Although a number of people attended his funeral, he suffered through a terminal illness without a close friend.

What is the cure for a poor self-image? It is to see ourselves from God's perspective. First, that means realizing that through Christ we *are* people of value. Ephesians

2:10 declares, "For we are His workmanship, created in Christ Jesus for good works." That verse implies that every facet of our beings—our looks, our abilities, our personalities—was ordained by God.

Second, we are the recipients of God's interest and friendship. Think about it. The Creator of the universe wants to have a relationship with *you*. He loved you enough that He was willing to lay down His life for you. Now that's friendship! Jesus said, "Greater love has no one than this, that one lay down his life for his friends" (John 15:13). The realization that God made us like we are and that He desires an intimate relationship with us should dispel doubts about our self-worth.

2. *Pride.* At the other end of the spectrum is another barrier to friendship: pride. As we saw in the last chapter, a deadly by-product of pride is independence. When we reach the erroneous conclusion that we are solely responsible for the good things in our lives, we are prone to feel that we do not need God or other people.

Such an attitude was a root cause of the trouble in the Corinthian church. A faulty understanding of spiritual gifts had led some of these Christians to believe that they had all of the gifts—or at least the most important gifts—so that they had no need for other believers. To correct this error, Paul compared the church to a physical body:

> But now there are many members, but one body. And the eye cannot say to the hand, "I have no need of you;" or again the head to the feet, "I have no need of you." On the contrary, it is much truer that members of the body which seem to be weaker are necessary . . . And if one member suffers, all the members suffer with it; if one member is honored, all the members rejoice with it. Now you are Christ's body and individually members of it" (1 Cor. 12:20-23; 26-27).

People are like the two porcupines that huddled together to keep warm. Pricked by each other's quills, they quickly moved apart. However, they soon began shivering again and had to move back together. They needed each other, even though they needled each other!

3. *Inability to accept others' faults.* When I was grow-ing up, my family would all often sit together to enjoy a Friday night movie—everyone except my younger brother. He could not stand to hear us crunching our popcorn, unwrapping our candy, or slurping our drinks. So he would go sit by himself in the front row of the theater. He was successful in escaping those obnoxious sounds. But the price he paid was one of isolation.

One reason people choose to be lonely is because of their unwillingness to accept the shortcomings of others. Companionship demands that we overlook other peoples' failures—just as God overlooks ours.

4. *Selfishness.* Another reason people sometimes opt out of companionship and "go it alone" is selfishness. In our culture, we use a euphemism for selfishness—busy-ness. "I'm just too busy for any close relationships." The truth is we choose how to spend our time, and we choose our level of activity. Good relationships cost something: time, emotional energy, effort, and sometimes pride. Some people are simply unwilling to make that investment. In their book *Friends and Friendship*, Jerry and Mary White state that the test of selflessness in friendship is "our re-sponse to a call for help." Would you . . .

... set aside personal interest to help?
... cancel a vacation to meet a pressing need?
... give money to help, even though you have little to give?
... spend exhausting time in prayer?
... accept others' children temporarily or even permanently?[4]

The next time you feel too busy to invest time in other people, remember the words of Philippians 2:3-4: "Do nothing from selfishness or empty conceit, but with humil-ity of mind let each of you regard one another as more important than himself; do not merely look out for your own personal interests, but also for the interests of others."

5. *Unwillingness to forgive others.* Friendships can sometimes be painful. Whenever we share ourselves with another, we run the risk of being hurt. Unfortunately, some people never recover from the inevitable disappointments that come from relationships. "I trusted somebody and look what happened. They . . .

  . . . divulged a confidence.
  . . . cheated me out of some money.
  . . . betrayed me.
  . . . refused to invite me to their party.
  . . . criticized me behind my back.

"I'll never let myself be burned like that again!" they vow. The result of such bitterness is often a lonely existence. Some years ago I received an unexpected letter from a friend. Noting the return address, I eagerly opened the letter to see what my friend had to say. I need not have been so eager. The typed letter, which ran several pages, was a detailed list of grievances this person had against me. The letter closed with, "I hope you won't take this *too* personally. Sincerely, _____." Not take it personally? I was so angry that I determined I would never have anything to do with my friend again. For several weeks I avoided him. But then the words of Matthew 5:23-24 came to mind: "If therefore you are presenting your offering at the altar, and there remember that your brother has something against you, leave your offering there before the altar, and go your way; first be reconciled to your brother, and then come and present your offering."

With those words in mind, I swallowed my pride and went to see this person. He said that it had been a bad day when he wrote the letter and said he was sorry. We talked matters over and a choice friendship was salvaged.

True friendship allows others to have a bad day. As the writer of Proverbs says, "A friend loves at *all* times [even when the other person is having a rough day!]" (17:17).

6. *Failure to understand the value of companionship.* Companionship is not a luxury; it is a necessity for our physical, emotional, and spiritual health. The magazine

Modern Maturity ran an article titled "You May Live Longer if You're Sociable" detailing the value of companionship. The article stated:

> In one of the most comprehensive studies of older adults ever undertaken in the United States—more than 20 years of interviews begun with 1,700 rural elderly in 64 culturally diverse towns in Missouri—researchers have determined that participation in formal social networks (church and community groups) is an even more important predictor of mortality than one's health.
>
> Richard Hessler, Ph.D., professor of sociology and family and community medicine at the University of Missouri-Columbia School of Medicine, says: "Regardless of health problems, people who had formal social networks in 1966 [when the study began] were more likely to remain independent and survive."
>
> In his landmark study of the physical and social changes involved in the aging process, the professor found four factors that most influenced whether a person lived or died during the research period: age, sex, health, and formal social networks, with the latter being foremost.[5]

Interpersonal relationships offer more than longevity of life. The Bible details both the emotional and spiritual benefits of companionship in Ecclesiastes, a little-read section of Scripture.

■ *It's Lonely at the Top*

Solomon had it all—power, wealth, pleasure, wisdom, stature—and yet, he had no one to share it with. Sure, he had 700 wives and 300 concubines, but his life was void of true intimacy. Solomon longed for companionship. Without it, he said, life is meaningless:

> Then I looked again at vanity under the sun. There was a certain man without a dependent, having neither son nor a brother, yet there was no end to all his

labor. Indeed his eyes were not satisfied with riches
and he never asked, "And for whom am I laboring and
depriving myself of pleasure?" This too is vanity and
it is a grievous task (Ecc. 4:7-8).

Such a realization led Solomon to make the following
observations about the value of companionship:

Two are better than one because they have a good
return for their labor. For if either of them falls, the
one will lift up his companion. But woe to the one
who falls when there is not another to lift him up.
Furthermore, if two lie down together they keep
warm, but how can one be warm alone? And if one
can overpower him who is alone, two can resist him.
A cord of three strands is not quickly torn apart (Ecc.
4:9-12).

Why are two better than one? What benefits does companionship offer?

1. *Assistance in times of crisis.* A popular Swedish
motto states: "Shared joy is a double joy. Shared sorrow is
half a sorrow." Solomon had this idea in mind when he
observed that a primary benefit of companionship was encouragement during a crisis: "For if either of them falls,
the one will lift up his companion." And friends rarely
"fall" at the same time. Have you ever noticed that often
one person in a relationship is "up" when the other person
is "down?" We can allow such incongruity of feelings to
hinder our relationships:

"Why are you so depressed? Cheer up and be like me!"

"Why are you so happy? If you were sensitive to my
feelings, you wouldn't be so light-hearted!"

Or, we can realize that God allows us to suffer crises at
different times so that we can support one another. Imagine two people simultaneously in quicksand. Neither
person would be in a position to help the other. Only
someone out of the mire would be able to offer a helping
hand. In the same way, relationships are important because they offer assistance in times of need.

2. *Support when we feel alone.* Remember the porcupine story? Maybe that is what Solomon had in mind when he observed, "If two lie down together they keep warm, but how can one be warm alone?" However, I think Solomon had more in mind than body temperature. As one writer observed, Solomon probably was thinking of the value of companionship in vulnerable situations like a move to a new city, the start of a new job, or the loss of a loved one.

The biblical story of Ruth and Naomi illustrates the value of companionship during times of loneliness. Ruth had lost her husband in death. Her mother-in-law Naomi, a widow herself, advised Ruth to return to her mother's house or find another husband. But Ruth was unwilling to sever the relationship. She realized that she needed Naomi and Naomi needed her, especially as they faced an uncertain future. Ruth's plea for her mother-in-law's companionship contains some of the most beautiful words in the Bible: "Do not urge me to leave you or turn back from following you; for where you go, I will go, and where you lodge, I will lodge. Your people shall be my people, and your God, my God" (Ruth 1:16).

The rest of the story reveals that Ruth and Naomi's relationship provided many benefits to both women and was instrumental in Ruth's entering into a marriage that would ultimately produce one of the forerunners of Christ.

3. *Protection when we are under siege.* Have you ever felt like the Apostle Paul? "Our flesh had no rest, but we were afflicted on every side: conflicts without, fears within" (2 Cor. 7:5). Paul was expressing a basic truth of life: we are constantly facing attack, whether it be from other people, circumstances, or even Satan. Solomon reminds us that companionship offers protection during such attacks: "And if one can overpower, two can resist him. A cord of three strands is not quickly torn apart" (Ecc. 4:12).

Sometimes other people can serve as our advocates when we are being mistreated. One of the occupational hazards of the ministry is criticism. How grateful I am to have friends within my congregation who are willing to defend me against unwarranted criticism and free me from the burden of having to defend myself.

Other times, those closest to us can provide us with perspective about our problems. At times, we are so overwhelmed by our problems that we need an objective, loving voice to say to us, "You know, as I look at your situation I believe that you are under spiritual attack. There is no other explanation for all that you are experiencing. I am going to pray that God will give you the spiritual strength to properly respond to this test."

Solomon says that it is harder to defeat two than one. And he adds that three are almost invincible. Some have suggested that the third person is a reference to Christ. Maybe. But more likely, Solomon is referring to the value of many friends. Do you have a small group of people with whom you can freely talk, pray, laugh, and even cry? Such relationships are invaluable during times of attack.[6]

4. *Accountability when we are prone to waver.* Recently I received a disturbing phone call. A longtime friend had fallen into gross immorality. When I first knew him in high school, he was very involved with our youth group. In college, many regarded him as a spiritual leader. But as he entered adulthood, he became so absorbed by materialism that he began drifting away from his spiritual moorings. He dropped out of church and began running with a different crowd. He had no responsible person to challenge his behavior. Thus his fall into immorality was quite easy.

That was the story of Solomon's life. His meteoric rise to the top left him with no one to be accountable to. Although he had been dedicated to God in his youth, materialism and sensual pleasure turned his heart away from God: "For it came about when Solomon was old, his wives turned his heart away after other gods; and his heart was not wholly devoted to the Lord His God, as the heart of David his father had been" (1 Kings 11:4). Yet no one dared to tell King Solomon the truth.

Who will tell you the truth about yourself? Who loves you enough to call your actions into question? Who is close enough to both you and God that they can sense when you are drifting spiritually? One of the prime benefits of companionship is accountability.

■ *Looking For Love in All the Right Places*

"All right, you've convinced me that close relationships are important. But where can I find those kind of relationships?" As I search through the Bible, I find at least three realms of relationships that God ordained to satisfy our need for intimacy:

1. *Marriage.* After God's crowning work of creating man, He said, "It is not good for the man to be alone" (Gen. 2:18). Alone? Adam was not alone. He was enjoying a perfect relationship with God—one that had not yet been tainted with sin. Yet God said that was not enough. Why?

Adam, like all of us, was a spiritual being. And therefore, he could not find ultimate contentment without a spiritual relationship with his Creator. But, like all of us, Adam was *more* than a spiritual being. He also needed an intimate relationship with another person. And God's primary way of satisfying that need was through the marriage relationship—giving him Eve.

Adam's and Eve's need for an intimate relationship with someone of the opposite sex was not unique to them. Moses closed this story with a general application for all of us: "For this cause a man shall leave his father and his mother, and shall cleave to his wife; and they shall become one flesh. And the man and his wife were both naked and were not ashamed" (Gen. 2:24-25).

God's plan for most people (except those with the special gift of celibacy) is that they find their deepest need for intimacy satisfied in a monogamous, heterosexual relationship that endures a lifetime.

2. *Friendships.* Marriage cannot satisfy all of our needs for companionship. As we have already seen, the Bible also places great value on friendships. There are at least four different levels of friendship:

a. *Acquaintances.* These are people you meet in the daily course of life: at the store, at work, in the neighborhood, or at church. One author has estimated that the average person makes anywhere from 500 to 2,500 acquaintances a year. Most of these relationships are superficial and will never evolve into anything deeper.

b. *Casual friends.* These are acquaintances that we

know on a first-name basis. We have continuing contact with them and may even socialize with them occasionally. Our conversation with these people usually involves superficial topics like the weather, sports, fashion, the stock market, or children. Such friendships may last for only months or they may span a lifetime.

c. *Close friends.* Depending on our social and work contacts, our close friends might number anywhere from five to twenty-five people. These people might include neighbors, church members, or work associates with whom we feel a special comradery. Such relationships are characterized by mutual agreement on many of the basic issues of life and a freedom to discuss personal feelings and concerns.

d. *Intimate friends.* A person usually has from one to a maximum of six truly intimate friends. These are people with whom we can share our deepest feelings with complete openness. An intimate friend is usually the first person we want to talk with in a crisis. Although the nature of such friendships can change, they most likely will endure a lifetime, regardless of geographical distance.[7]

An understanding of the different levels of friendship can keep us from one of the most potent dangers in relationships: unrealistic expectations. For example, when we expect casual friends to behave like intimate friends, we are bound to be disappointed. We need to understand that God brings different people into our lives for differing purposes. I like what Ted Engstrom, former president of World Vision, says about different kinds of friendships: "Every Christian . . . needs a Barnabas to receive encouragement, a Timothy to guide as a protege; and an Epaphroditus to enjoy on a peer level."

3. *Relationships in the church.* Friendships may involve both non-Christians (remember, Jesus was known as a friend of sinners) and Christians. Furthermore, our friendships with believers may (and should!) cross ecclesiastical boundaries. But God has created a third realm for satisfying our need for companionship—the local church. Although we find all four levels of friendship in the local church, there is a collective power of those relationships

that provides us with the spiritual encouragement we need to stand firm in our relationship with God.

We preachers love to quote Hebrews 10:25—"not forsaking our own assembling together, as is the habit of some"—to shame our members into more regular church attendance. But when you look at the context of that verse, you will find that the motivation for regular church attendance was not to satisfy some legalistic requirement, but to meet a legitimate spiritual need: "Let us consider how to stimulate one another to love and good deeds, not forsaking our own assembling together, as is the habit of some, but encouraging one another; and all the more, as you see the day drawing near" (Heb. 10:24-25).

Have you ever noticed a piece of wood in a fireplace? When it is placed in the middle of the fire, it glows red hot. But take the wood out of the fire, and the wood turns from red, to orange, to gray, and then finally coal black. But place it back into the fire, and it will start to glow again. A Christian is like that piece of wood. He needs the rest of the "embers" to ignite him and keep him glowing red hot!

■ We Need Each Other

"Hell is other people." That is what Jean-Paul Sarte, the architect of French existentialism, wrote on one occasion. Sure, relationships can be a nuisance at times, but they are necessary for our fulfillment. Dr. Louis Leakey, his wife Mary, and their son Richard dedicated their lives to studying the habits of chimpanzees. On one occasion they wrote, "One chimpanzee is no chimpanzee." In other words, it is only in the company of other chimpanzees that a chimp fully develops. Isolated, a chimp never reaches its full potential.[8]

What is true of chimps is even more true of us. God has designed us in such a way that we desperately need other people. Sarte was wrong. Hell is loneliness. But companionship is the cornerstone of God's plan for life.

CHAPTER TWELVE

CHOOSING INTIMACY WITH GOD OVER ISOLATION

*"Remember also your Cre-
ator in the days of your
youth, before the evil days
come and the years draw
near when you will say, 'I
have no delight in them.' "*
Ecc. 12:1

■ A few years ago, I had one of my most embarrassing
experiences in the ministry. I had been invited to Canada
to speak at a church banquet. The plane landed in Winnipeg around 4 P.M. After claiming my luggage, I stood outside the terminal waiting for the pastor who was to meet
me. Thirty minutes passed—no pastor.

As I glanced at his original letter, I noticed that the city
and province on the return address did not correspond to
my present location! Because I had once preached for the
pastor at his church in Winnipeg, I had assumed he was
still there. I took the return address to the airline counter,
explaining that I had apparently come to the wrong city. I
told him that I really wanted to be in Vancouver. Not knowing much about Canada, I innocently asked, "Is there a bus
I can catch? I'm supposed to speak there in a few hours."

"A bus?" They all laughed. "Vancouver, British Colum-
bia is 1,500 miles from here!"

As a pastor, I have had to make many difficult phone

calls—but none has ever approached the call I had to make to that preacher! Fortunately, the story had a happy ending. The airline personnel were able to put me on a plane that was immediately departing for Vancouver. Even though it was a three-hour flight, the time change traveling west allowed me to arrive in time to speak. As I was boarding the flight, the ticket agent handed me a map of Canada and chuckled, "Here, read this; it might help you next time!"

Maps are certainly important for giving direction. But, the only thing worse than having no map is having the *wrong* map. Stephen Covey writes about the importance of having a correct map in his book *Seven Habits of Highly Effective People:*

> Suppose you wanted to arrive at a specific location in central Chicago. A street map of the city would be a great help to you in reaching your destination. But suppose you were given the wrong map. Through a printing error, the map labeled "Chicago" was actually a map of Detroit. Can you imagine the frustration, the ineffectiveness of trying to reach your destination?
>
> You might work on your behavior—you could try harder, be more diligent, double your speed. But your efforts would only succeed in getting you to the wrong place faster.
>
> You might work on your attitude—you could think more positively. You still wouldn't get to the right place, but perhaps you wouldn't care. Your attitude would be so positive, you'd be happy wherever you were.
>
> The point is, you'd still be lost. The fundamental problem has nothing to do with your behavior or your attitude. It has everything to do with having a wrong map[1].

The problem with most motivational books—yes, even "Christian" motivational books—is that they deal with such topics as perseverance, goals, attitudes, and interpersonal skills, without giving the reader the proper "map" by which to chart such behavior. By a "map" I mean a way of viewing life. For example, a geographical map gives you a proper perspective and helps you get from Point A to Point B. It is a model of geographical realities.

In the same way, we all have mental "maps" about life by which we formulate our behavior and values. Are we free to develop our own mental maps? Of course we are. But imagine the folly of deciding you were going to develop your own map of Chicago, based on your feelings about how you would like the city to be arranged. Such a map would be extremely inaccurate and, as a result, would be of little help in giving direction.

In this final chapter, we will examine the most basic attitude choice in life—*a choice that results in a proper mental "map" of life*. All other attitude choices we make should be built on the foundational decision of choosing intimacy with God.

■ *Journal of a Playboy*

Thousands of years ago there lived a man who was searching for the meaning of life. The endless cycles of human life and nature had led this man to conclude that life "under the sun" was utterly meaningless. Yet the wisest man that ever lived was not content to draw his conclusions about the value of life from nature alone. So, Solomon set out on a personal pilgrimage to discover the proper "map" that would give direction to his life: "I, the Preacher, have been king over Israel in Jerusalem. And I set my mind to seek and explore by wisdom concerning all that has been done under heaven. (Ecc. 1:12-13).

The rest of the book of Ecclesiastes is a record of Solomon's exploration of the meaning of life. Solomon tried a number of different maps to discover a purpose for living. Let's look at several of the wrong maps Solomon utilized:

Map #1: Pleasure. Solomon's first guide for discovering the meaning of life was pleasure. He would examine every source of pleasure to try to discover purpose in life: "I said to myself, 'Come now, I will test you with pleasure. So enjoy yourself.' And behold, it too was futility" (Ecc.

2:1). He tried laughter, wine, houses, wealth, and sex. But none of those things satisfied. His conclusion? "I denied myself nothing my eyes desired; I refused my heart no pleasure. . . . Yet when I surveyed all that my hands had done and what I had toiled to achieve, everything was meaningless, a chasing after the wind; nothing was gained under the sun" (2:10-11, NIV).

Map #2: Wisdom. Disappointed with the emptiness of pleasure, Solomon tried another "map" to give direction to his life: wisdom. Solomon had always placed a premium on wisdom. He was really more of a thinker than a playboy at heart. When he was twenty, God promised to give him anything he wanted. What did he ask for? Most twenty-year-old men would have asked for a flashy concubine or the latest model chariot. But not Solomon. He asked for wisdom. And God answered his request by making him the wisest man who ever lived. While Solomon valued wisdom over foolishness, he realized its limitations: "But I came to realize that the same fate overtakes them. . . . Like the fool, the wise man too must die!" (2:14, 16, NIV).

Death, Solomon discovered, is the great leveler of us all. In the cemetery, there are both wise and foolish men. The wise may be buried in Westminster Abbey, while the fools are in unmarked graves. But does it really matter? Dead is dead.

Thus Solomon concluded, " 'The fate of the fool will overtake me also. What then do I gain by being wise?' I said in my heart, 'This too is meaningless' " (2:15, NIV).

Map #3: Work. If pleasure or wisdom did not provide lasting joy, Solomon decided that maybe work was the answer. Like many of us today, he tried worshiping at the shrine of vocation. But this too proved futile. Why? One very practical reason is found in 2:18-19: "I hated all the things I had toiled for under the sun, because I must leave them to the one who comes after me. And who knows whether he will be a wise man or a fool? Yet he will have control over all the work into which I have poured my effort and skill under the sun. This too is meaningless" (NIV).

That's a sobering thought! Everything you work for will

someday be turned over to someone else. And who knows how they will manage it?

When my father discovered he had terminal cancer, he wanted to make sure all his affairs were in order. I will never forget sitting at the kitchen table with him as he detailed the location of his different assets. Suddenly, he stopped, looked over at me, and grinned. "This is so ironic. I have worked and saved all of my life for my old age, and now I am going to end up leaving it all to someone else!" That's the wisdom that death brings.

I think Solomon had his own experience in mind when he penned these words. After building Israel into a strong and wealthy nation, Solomon turned over the reins of power to his son, Rehoboam. In less than a year, Rehoboam destroyed the country by a series of bad decisions, plunging the nation into civil war.

But even if your work continues to prosper after you are gone, it will be of no consequence to you. Why? Because you will not be here to enjoy it. It is folly to sell your soul to your work, because ultimately you are going to die.

This is the truth that Jesus illustrated in Luke 12:16-21:

And He told them a parable, saying, "The land of a certain rich man was very productive. And he began reasoning to himself, saying, 'What shall I do, since I have no place to store my crops?' And he said, 'This is what I will do: I will tear down my barns and build larger ones, and there I will store all my grain and my goods. And I will say to my soul, "Soul, you have many goods laid up for many years to come; take your ease, eat, drink, and be merry." But God said to him, 'You fool! This very night your soul is required of you; and now who will own what you have prepared?' So is the man who lays up treasure for himself, and is not rich toward God."

It really does not matter what treasure you are spending your life to acquire: pleasure, wisdom, or wealth. Solomon and Jesus both affirmed the foolishness of trading the eternal for the temporal.

■ *Life above the Sun*

The first eleven chapters of Ecclesiastes record Solomon's attempt to find the right "map" to give purpose and order to his life. As a result, he found that pleasure is futile, wisdom is vain, work is meaningless, government is corrupt, life is unfair, and death awaits us all.

Life *is* meaningless "under the sun" — a phrase Solomon uses twenty-nine times in Ecclesiastes. This phrase denotes the limited perspective with which Solomon viewed life. Life under the sun is a life apart from God. It is only when we view life above the sun that we gain a clearer perspective.

Possibly you have had the experience of boarding an aircraft on a cloudy, rainy day. As the plane rolls down the runway, the rain streaks across the window. But in a few moments, the plane soars above those gray clouds into the sunlight. Under the clouds, the outlook is dreary. Above the clouds, everything looks radiant.

The final chapter of Ecclesiastes records Solomon's "above the sun" perspective: "Remember also your Creator in the days of your youth, before the evil days come and years draw near when you will say, 'I have no delight in them' " (12:1). Solomon, after years of empty pursuits, concluded that the only proper map to chart a life by is one that has God at the center. That is the idea of the word translated "remember." It does not mean simply to acknowledge the existence of someone. The word has the idea of action.

For example, when God "remembered" Hannah (1 Sam. 1:19), He did more than say, "Oh yes, Hannah; I almost forgot you." When He remembered her, He acted decisively on her behalf, and she who was barren conceived the child Samuel. So it is in our passage. To remember our Creator calls for decisive action based on recollection and reflection on all that God is and has done for us.[2]

I believe that the "decisive action" Solomon has in mind is that of developing an intimate relationship with God. Solomon is saying that life's most important attitude choice is to build one's existence around God. How is that accomplished? I believe there are four vital steps to developing an intimate relationship with God:

1. *Realize that true fulfillment is impossible apart from God.* Divided affections block intimacy in any relationship. Just as it would be impossible for me to achieve emotional oneness with my wife while also being involved with another woman, it is impossible for us to develop intimacy with God while depending on something or someone else to satisfy our needs. I believe that is what Jesus meant when He warned, "No one can serve two masters; for either he will hate the one and love the other, or he will hold to one and despise the other. You cannot serve God and Mammon" (Matt. 6:24).

We tend to worship that which we think will satisfy our needs. Thus when we operate under the illusion that people, power, possessions, prestige, or anything else is the answer to our deepest desires, we will forsake our relationship with God. And the first eleven chapters of Ecclesiastes is Solomon's eyewitness testimony that none of those things is worthy of our affections.

In the second chapter of this book, I wrote about the importance of setting goals—choosing purpose in life over aimlessness. Recently, I discovered a piece of paper on which I had written four major goals for my life eight years ago. As I reflected on those goals, I was pleased that I had both achieved and surpassed them. But did such an accomplishment satisfy me? Of course not! In the past eight years, I have set dozens of other goals. And I will continue to do so. If the achievement of those goals could really satisfy, why would I need more?

I believe Solomon had reached the same conclusion. All of his goals had been realized—he was the richest, wisest, most powerful monarch in the world. Yet at the end of his life he had concluded it was all meaningless. Not only were such goals empty, but they had robbed him of the one pursuit that could have satisfied him—an intimate relationship with God.

2. *Honestly evaluate your relationship with God.* Where are your affections centered right now? Having difficulty determining that? Then imagine that you were to suddenly lose everything of value to you—your family,

your job, your reputation, your money, and your health. What would be your response? Beyond the normal mourning over such a loss, would you lose all reason for living? Would your life spin hopelessly out of control?

We have the record of a man who suffered such a loss. Remember Job? In a relatively short period of time, he lost everything. Yet, his reaction was nothing short of remarkable: "Then Job arose and tore his robe and shaved his head, and he fell to the ground and worshiped. And he said, 'Naked I came from my mother's womb, and naked I shall return there. The Lord gave and the Lord has taken away. Blessed be the name of the Lord.' Through all this Job did not sin nor did he blame God" (Job 1:20-22).

Make no mistake about it—Job grieved over his loss. But he was still able to worship. Why? Because the object of his worship was still intact. Unlike many of us, Job had not fallen into the trap of worshiping the gifts instead of the Giver of the gifts. In the midst of great upheaval, the foundation of Job's life remained firm.

What a contrast to Solomon! The twelfth chapter of Ecclesiastes paints a portrait of an old man whose life is beginning to unravel. His health is broken ("the silver cord is broken . . . the golden bowl is crushed . . . the pitcher by the well is shattered"), his power has been diminished, his wealth has been passed on to another, and even his wisdom has been called into question. Such a pathetic conclusion to life leads Solomon to advise, "Remember your Creator in the days of your youth." I think such advice could be paraphrased, "Put God first in your life before it is too late."

Have you ever been on a trip to an unfamiliar destination and made a wrong turn? After a few miles, you realize your mistake. At this point, the logical thing to do is to turn around. But if you are like me, you hate to admit your mistake and backtrack a number of miles. So you keep going in the wrong direction, thinking that, just possibly, the wrong way will magically turn out to be the right way. Of course, the farther you go in the wrong direction, the harder it is to finally turn around.

An honest evaluation of your relationship with God

necessitate a change in the direction of your life. That is the concept behind the word *repent* which means to have a change of mind or to change direction. If you see that your affections have not been centered around God, admit your mistake and change direction, before it is too difficult for you to make such a change.

Unfortunately, Solomon apparently had traveled too far in his pursuit of pleasure, power, and possession to turn around. The sad epitaph of Israel's most powerful monarch is recorded in 1 Kings 11:4, "For it came about when Solomon was old, his wives turned his heart away after other gods; and his heart was not wholly devoted to the Lord his God, as the heart of David his father had been." And yet Solomon desired that we learn from his tragic mistake: "Remember your Creator—put God first in your life—before it is too late."

3. *Remove any barriers to intimacy with God.* What is hindering your relationship with God? While a variety of answers are possible, I believe all such excuses can be boiled down to the "S" word—sin. The Prophet Isaiah said, "But your iniquities have made a separation between you and your God . . . " (59:2). We usually think of sin in terms of certain actions—lying, stealing, murdering, etc. But such actions stem from a basic attitude choice—doing what we want to do, instead of what God wants us to do. Such an attitude, along with the accompanying actions, builds a wall between us and God. How can such a wall be torn down?

From God's perspective, the wall is removed when we admit our sin and turn to Jesus Christ for forgiveness. But as I explained in chapter 5, we continue to sin, even after we have been forgiven. Although such sin does not change God's attitude toward us, it does change our attitude toward God, causing another barrier to intimacy with God.

Of all the sins that Christians commit, none seems to block intimacy with God any more than idolatry. Before you breathe a sigh of relief and convince yourself that this is one sin of which you are not guilty, let me explain what I mean by idolatry. This sin is not limited to bowing down before a wooden deity in the darkest jungle of Africa. Idolatry is the attitude of depending on someone or something other than God to satisfy our deepest needs. And before we can ever hope to develop an intimate relationship with God, we must not only identify idols in our lives, we must also remove them.

Recently, I was eating lunch with a widely known Christian leader. This teacher is familiar to millions of Americans. Yet, despite his fame, he lives a very frugal existence. Of particular interest to me was the car he was driving—a 1968 Oldsmobile. When I asked him about his car, he began to point out the merits of the car. "It's economical, it's safe (they don't build them like that anymore), and I certainly don't have to worry about anyone stealing it!" I probed a little further, asking about the philosophy behind his simple lifestyle.

He related a story from his childhood. When he was ten years old, he had a paper route which produced an impressive sum of money. Every week, he deposited his earnings in the local bank. He took great pride in the amount of money he had accumulated. However, he soon began to realize that his bank book had become the center of his affections. As God began to speak to him, he knew what he must do. He went to the bank, withdrew all of the money, and purchased Bibles for his classmates. From that point on, he said, he has never had a problem with materialism.

Whatever barrier is blocking our relationship with God— idolatry, bitterness, unresolved guilt, envy, lust—we must be willing to take the same kind of drastic action that boy took to maintain our intimacy with God.

4. *Continue to nurture your relationship with God.* Here is a formula guaranteed to destroy any relationship:

a. Don't ever talk to the other person.

b. Don't ever listen to the other person.

c. Make sure you are always too busy to spend time with the other person.

Unfortunately, many of us are in the process of unintentionally destroying the relationships that are most important to us. We assume that our marriage, our friendship and our relationships with our children will remain str simply because they started out strong. Yet the truth i' all relationships take nurturing to remain healthy.

The last several months around our house have been hectic, to say the least. A full schedule at our church, travel commitments, and publishing deadlines kept me from spending some quality time with my wife. Several weeks ago I was supposed to take her out to lunch before I left on a long trip. Something came up at the church, and I had to cancel the lunch. I ran into the house, grabbed my bags, and started to head for the airport, when my wife asked, "Robert, where is your calendar?"

"It's in my desk drawer. Why do you want to know?" I asked.

"Because I want to make an appointment to see you like everyone else does. How about next Tuesday at 11 A.M.?"

I got the message. I had been neglecting the most important relationship in my life—not because I wanted to, but because I assumed since it was my most stable relationship, I could neglect it without any serious consequences. *Wrong!*

I came back from my trip with a new determination to set aside a regular time each day to talk with my wife—not out of duty, but out of a desire to maintain intimacy with her. I am amazed how quickly we can grow distant from each other. Just a few days of no meaningful communication leads to a feeling of isolation.

If that is true in the marriage relationship, how much more true it is in our relationship with God! How could we hope to maintain a relationship with Someone we can't even see, without working to nurture such a relationship?

How do we maintain intimacy with God? You know all of the answers: talking with God (prayer); letting God talk with you (Bible study); worship; Scripture memory; etc. But let me share with you one practice that has done more to strengthen my relationship with God than any other: keeping a spiritual journal. My spiritual journal is simply a record of my relationship with God. The first few pages of this spiral notebook are dedicated to prayer requests. I have divided the page into two columns: My Requests and God's Answers.

I list each prayer request and date it under the heading

My Request. Then, when the answer comes—whatever the answer is—I describe it under the heading God's Answers and date it. I have pages and pages filled with miraculous answers to prayer that constantly remind me that God really is alive and in the business of hearing the requests of His children. By the way, I have plenty of "no" answers too. God has shown me the wisdom of some of those negative answers; I will have to trust Him about the others. But what an encouragement it is to thumb through those pages and see how God has worked in my life over the years!

The rest of my journal is a record of my relationship with God. Every day I write a brief paragraph or a page describing what God is teaching me, what struggles I am encountering, or verses in the Bible that have spoken to me. Although keeping a spiritual journal does not take more than twenty minutes a day, this discipline, coupled with prayer and Bible study, can keep your relationship with God alive and vibrant.

■ *Shadows and Substance*

The Book of Ecclesiastes was Solomon's spiritual journal. And he opened its pages to us so that we might profit from it. Solomon's spiritual journal led him to the conclusion that purpose in life could not be found in pleasure, work, wealth, or even wisdom.

One of my favorite fables is about the dog who crossed a bridge while carrying a bone in his mouth. The dog happened to glance over the edge of the bridge to see the reflection of the bone in the pool below. Not realizing it was only a reflection, the dog dropped his bone and plunged into the water in pursuit of the reflection. The dog dropped the substance in his mouth for the shadow, and went hungry.

Solomon made the mistake of dropping the substance for the shadow. The result of his decision was isolation from God and an insatiable spiritual hunger. The wisest man who ever lived reminds us that the most important attitude choice in life is to choose intimacy with God over isolation.

PERSONAL AND
GROUP STUDY GUIDE

Before beginning your personal or group study of
Choose Your Attitudes, Change Your Life, **take time to
read these introductory comments.**

If you are working through the study on your own, you
may want to adapt certain sections (for example, the ice-
breakers), and record your responses to all questions in a
separate notebook. You might find it more enriching or
motivating to study with a partner with whom you can
share answers or insights.

If you are leading a group, you may want to ask your group
members to read each assigned chapter and work through
the study questions before the group meets. This isn't
always easy for busy adults, so encourage them with occa-
sional phone calls or notes between meetings. Help members manage their time by pointing out how they can cover
a few pages each day. Also have them identify a regular
time of the day or week that they can devote to the study.
They too may write their responses to the questions in
notebooks.

Notice that each session includes the following features:

Session Topic—a brief statement summarizing the session.
Icebreaker—an activity to help group members get better
acquainted with the session topic and/or with each other.
Group Discovery Questions—a list of questions to encourage individual discovery or group participation.
Personal Application Questions—an aid to applying the
knowledge gained through study to one's personal living.
(Note: These are important questions for group members
to answer for themselves, even if they do not wish to discuss their responses in the meeting.)

Optional Activities — supplemental ideas that will enhance the study.

Prayer Focus — suggestions for turning one's learning into prayer.

Assignment — activities or preparation to complete prior to the next session.

Here are a few tips which can help you more effectively lead small group studies:

Pray for each group member, asking the Lord to help you create an open atmosphere where everyone will feel free to share with one another and you.

Encourage group members to bring their Bibles as well as their texts to each session. This study is based on the *New International Version*, but it is good to have several translations on hand for purposes of comparison.

Start and end on time. This is especially important for the first meeting because it will set the pattern for the rest of the sessions.

Begin with prayer, asking the Holy Spirit to open hearts and minds and to give understanding so that truth will be applied.

Involve everyone. As learners, we retain only 10% of what we hear; 20% of what we see; 65% of what we hear and see; but 90% of what we hear, see, and do.

Promote a relaxed environment. Arrange the chairs in a circle or semicircle. This allows eye contact among members and encourages dynamic discussion. Be relaxed in your own attitude and manner. Be willing to share yourself.

CHAPTER ONE

ATTITUDE IS EVERYTHING

Session Topic: We can be transformed into what God intends us to be through choosing certain attitudes in our life circumstances.

Icebreakers *(Choose one)*

1. New Year's resolutions are often difficult to keep. Share a resolution you have made and how you fared with it.
2. The author states that "to a large extent, our attitudes are shaped by external influences." What do you think is the strongest external influence for adults today?

Group Discovery Questions

1. Do you believe it is possible to purposefully change your "mental or emotional responses to the circumstances of life"? (See Phil. 2:5; 4:8.) By what means do you think a person could accomplish this?
2. Why is change necessary? What is the goal of our making the 11 essential attitude choices listed by the author?
3. How does the author differentiate his ideas from the "name it and claim it" positive thinking philosophies?
4. Review the listed scriptural references to the importance of right thinking. What does it mean to have your mind renewed? How is this related to choosing certain attitudes?
5. How is it true that "our attitudes are both the cause and the result of right behavior"?
6. What is the one attitude that pleases God as we encounter the universal circumstance of sin? Find a Scripture for this. Why will this affect where you spend eternity?

Personal Application Questions

1. As you consider the topic of this book, are you more aware of the attitude choices which you have? If so, how has this increased awareness affected you?
2. Are you able to see any ways in which your character has become more similar to the character of Jesus Christ? To what do you attribute this change?

3. Of the attitude choices listed, with which do you feel most successful? Least successful?

4. Do you believe you have the unlimited power of the Holy Spirit to aid you in your resolutions? If so, is that power a reality in your day-to-day life? For encouragement, look up other references to the power and work of the Holy Spirit in a believer's life.

5. Which external influences can you eliminate and which can you add for the purpose of influencing correct attitudes?

6. What are some right actions you can institute in order to have the right attitudes in your most troublesome relationship?

7. Have you had an attitude of repentance concerning your sin? If so, claim the promise of 1 John 1:9.

Optional Activities

1. Make a list of situations and/or relationships in which you have difficulty with your attitude. Next to each, write the wrong attitude you struggle with and the attitude you know you should choose. Monitor your progress.

2. If you are anticipating roadblocks in your attitude choices, talk it over with a friend and devise a plan of action which will help you in your most difficult moments.

3. Post a list of the 11 attitude resolutions in a handy place where you can read them aloud each morning.

Prayer Focus

Ask God to continue His transforming work within you as you begin to take charge of your attitudes. Thank Him for the power of the Holy Spirit to keep the resolutions.

Assignment

1. When you feel wrong attitudes cropping up this week (and they most certainly will), try to consciously choose to have a positive attitude. Note any difficulties and consider what you need to do to be more successful in this area.

2. Read chapter 2 of the text and be sure to leave plenty of time to carefully work through the guided process of choosing a life purpose, objectives and goals. Then work through the corresponding study.

CHAPTER TWO

CHOOSING PURPOSE OVER AIMLESSNESS

Session Topic: Our lives will take on meaning when we choose a purpose, objectives, and goals for ourselves.

Icebreakers *(Choose one)*
1. Suppose a married couple wants to take a vacation next year at this time. What kinds of preparations and decisions will they need to make in order to have a successful trip?
2. The author states that only 3% of Americans today have clearly defined life goals. Do you know such a person? If so, what seems to characterize his or her living?

Group Discovery Questions
1. What does the author mean by "purpose" in life?
2. Read Philippians 2:13 from the Phillips translation (and if possible, other translations too). What are the implications for those who seek purpose in life?
3. How does the author describe a life purpose statement, objectives, and goals? Be sure to make distinctions between the three.
4. How could accountability to a partner help you establish and pursue your goals?
5. Why do you think many people fail to make specific goals for their lives, even when the advantages of doing so are evident?
6. Read the Phillips translation of Ephesians 5:15-17 which opens chapter 2 of the text. What is "the meaning and purpose of life"? Why is the believer who makes the most of his or her time more than merely an efficiency expert?
7. What kinds of everyday things waste the time that we should be wisely using?

Personal Application Questions
1. When you consider where you are in life today, would you say that you arrived there more by following a predetermined plan, or more by accident?
2. In answering the six questions suggested by Bob Biehl

for identifying the needs you feel strongly about, what did you notice that surprised you the most?

3. Did you find that the questions for identifying your gifts were helpful in narrowing down an area in which you are both interested and gifted? If so, how did you feel when you wrote down that specific area? If not, what is most difficult in identifying that area?

4. Does it seem yet that having a purpose statement will make a difference in your life?

5. What was the hardest part of formulating objectives for the seven major areas of your life?

6. How confident are you that all of your goals will be met? How will you react if very few of them are met? What can you do to increase the chances that goals will be met?

Optional Activities

1. Create a chart with your purpose statement across the top and your objectives and goals below. Place it in a handy spot in your home; check off the goals as you achieve them and move toward your objectives.

2. Do a topical study on the word *plan* in the Bible by using your concordance and cross-references. (Verses to begin with are Proverbs 15:22; 16:9; Psalm 37:23; James 4:13-15). Or do a study on biblical characters who reached objectives by making and completing goals. For example, Joseph before the famine in Egypt, Genesis 41:28-40; or Nehemiah as he led the reconstruction of the Jerusalem walls, in the Book of Nehemiah.

Prayer Focus

Thank God that He gives you purpose and a reason for living. Ask Him to help you understand His will as you formulate and pursue your life purpose, objectives, and goals.

Assignment

1. Make personal observations over the coming weeks on how your new purpose statement, objectives, and goals help you make everyday choices.

2. Read chapter 3 of the text and work through the corresponding study.

CHAPTER THREE

CHOOSING PERSEVERANCE OVER DEFEAT

Session Topic: Persisting in the pursuit of your goals in spite of the inevitable obstacles will likely result in success.

Icebreakers *(Choose one)*

1. There are many stories of famous people who found success by persevering in spite of incredible obstacles. Who is your favorite example and why?

2. Consider the example of the hardships in Abraham Lincoln's life. When do you think would have been an understandable time for Lincoln to accept defeat and live a life of mediocrity?

Group Discovery Questions

1. Why is perseverance an important element in the choice of purpose over aimlessness?

2. What does the author say will be the measure of your success in achieving your goals?

3. Is there a difference in the success rate of secular and Christian positive thinkers? Why or why not? Are there differing definitions of success?

4. Since every goal is not necessarily worthy of perseverance, how can we know which ones to continue pursuing? Is it ever right to quit?

5. What was the purpose of Israel's marching around Jericho? What kept them marching?

6. The author defines faith as "the confidence that God will do what He said He will do." Read also Hebrews 11:1. How does this relate to perseverance in our present-day goals?

7. What is your response to the statement that "people do not differ significantly in ability"? How might this affect how a parent would view and respond to his or her children?

Personal Application Questions

1. What is your characteristic response to obstacles placed in your way? Think of one example where you re-

gret your response and one where you are pleased with your response.

2. How did you feel after reading the summary of Lincoln's life story? Do you think you would have persevered if you were in his situation? What might his example inspire you to try or try again?

3. Examine your goals from the last chapter in light of the author's three criteria for determining if goals are worthy of pursuit. How do they hold up?

4. What obstacles do you anticipate for these same goals? How can you work to remove them or persist in spite of them?

5. Have you ever had to persevere through what seemed like meaningless steps in order to achieve a goal? Does meditating on God's Word sometimes seem meaningless to you? What sustains you during these times?

6. Think of an instance where you failed. How did this affect your goal? If you had it to do over again, what would you do differently?

7. If you could choose one accomplishment for your lifetime, what would it be? Does knowing this would take hard work discourage you from taking it on?

Optional Activities

1. Consider whether you would like to modify or add any goals after this encouragement that success often comes after persevering through obstacles and failure.

2. Interview several Christians you admire and ask them what role perseverance has played in their lives (or have group members share this with each other).

Prayer Focus

Thank God for the marvelous way He accomplishes His work and will in your life and ask Him to show you how to respond to the obstacles and failures that come your way.

Assignment

1. Memorize Joshua 1:8.

2. Read chapter 4 of the text and work through the corresponding study.

CHAPTER FOUR

CHOOSING FAITH OVER WORRY

Session Topic: "Peace of mind is available to anyone who will choose faith in God over anxiety" (author).

Icebreakers *(Choose one)*

1. Choose two people to do a role play in which one speaks and acts out the attitude of faith and one the attitude of anxiety in the following scenario. Your teenage daughter's curfew is 11:00 p.m. and it is now 11:45 p.m. and she is still not home.

2. What is the item that causes the most worry to you, the telephone, the clock, or the calendar?

Group Discovery Questions

1. Do you agree that worry is "the emotion of our age"? What are the signs or symptoms of worry and anxiety in our society today?

2. How can worry hinder a person's spiritual growth?

3. Is loving concern different from worry? In what way? How can we be healthily attached to someone but not be "building our lives" around them?

4. Do most people consciously choose to worry? Why does worry come so naturally?

5. What are some ways a person can rid themselves of anxiety once they have begun to feel it? Start with Philippians 4:6-7.

6. In the example of Daniel's response to King Darius' edict, do you think Daniel was not fearful at all? How do you think he was feeling?

7. Can God use for our good all anxiety, even the anxiety that is the result of Satanic attack? How can we cooperate in this process?

Personal Application Questions

1. What were the three greatest fears you listed in the book? Are you hanging "very heavy weights on very thin wires"?

2. Is any of your anxiety the result of sinful behavior?

3. Are you aware of times when God used your anxiety to bring you into a right relationship with Himself? Explain.
4. Would you say that most of the time your mind is set on the things above or the things that are on earth? (Col. 3:1-2)
5. Has recounting God's past faithfulness to you ever helped in alleviating your anxiety? If so, recall one example.
6. When you are anxious, what do you do and what are you thinking about? Is remaining in contact with God during anxious moments an automatic or an unlikely response to you?

Optional Activities
1. Keep a journal of prayer requests and answers so you will have a tangible record of God's faithfulness to you. When choosing faith is difficult, this will be an encouragement to you.
2. Share with someone what you worry about the most, and explain to them how you are working toward choosing faith over anxiety in that relationship or situation.

Prayer Focus
Thank God for the peace that is found through faith and ask Him to help you resist Satan and your own worldly worries and to grant you the faith necessary to chase away anxiety.

Assignment
1. This week when anxiety strikes, do the following.
If it is because of sin, repent.
If not because of sin, remove unnecessary fear by:
  • confronting the source,
  • confronting the truth,
  • remembering God's past faithfulness, and
  • remaining in contact with God.
   If needed post this plan of action where you can review it.
2. Read chapter 5 of the text and work through the corresponding study.

CHAPTER FIVE

CHOOSING REPENTANCE OVER GUILT

Session Topic: It is important for our physical, emotional, and spiritual health that we not ignore our moral failure but instead confront it and repent.

Icebreakers (Choose one)
1. Which is easier for you to do, to forgive or to forget?
2. Imagine that you have borrowed class notes from a friend in order to catch up on some material that you missed while you were ill. A week later you realize that you have lost the notes. You have seen this friend a couple times lately, and he has not yet asked for the notes back. You will be seeing this friend again this afternoon. What will you do?

Group Discovery Questions
1. What is repentance?
2. In the story of David and Bathsheba, what was the result of David's choice of ignoring his moral failures instead of repenting?
3. Do people ever really "get away with it" after doing wrong?
4. What is the difference between false guilt and true guilt? Which is the most prevalent? Is there a difference between guilt and guilt feelings?
5. Sometimes we can feel sorry about something without really repenting. In these instances, what is missing?
6. According to 2 Corinthians 7:10, "the sorrow of the world produces death." What does this mean?
7. What are some spiritual consequences of unresolved guilt?
8. How can we develop an attitude of repentance?

Personal Application Questions
1. How often do you have an attitude of repentance? When is the last time you acknowledged your failure and had a change in direction?
2. Is guilt a frequent visitor in your life? What symptoms

do you notice when you are feeling guilty?

3. On a continuum from "feel guilty too often" to "don't feel guilty often enough," where would you place yourself?

4. Has ignoring your moral failure (as David did) ever proved to result in even worse consequences? How did you eventually resolve the situation?

5. What is one sin that you feel sorry about but over which you have not really repented? What holds you back form repenting? Will you repent today?

6. Has guilt ever broken a relationship of yours? What did you do (or can you do) to restore that relationship?

7. In the section "Developing an Attitude of Repentance," you were asked to probe your life for ways you have failed to meet God's standards. What are the positive actions you are going to take to correct those failures?

8. If you have fully repented, you do not need to feel guilty any longer. Is there an area of your life in which it is difficult to accept God's forgiveness? Talk to someone about it and believe God's promise of 1 John 1:9.

Optional Activities

1. To emphasize God's forgiving and forgetting of those sins we have repented of, write down on paper a list of those sins which seem to be clinging to you. Then, for a visual reminder that they are really gone, safely burn the list. Alternately, you may want to erase them from a blackboard or nail the paper list to a hand-made wooden cross.

2. Memorize 1 John 1:9.

Prayer Focus

Pray Psalm 139:23-24: "Search me, O God, and know my heart; try me and know my anxious thoughts; and see if there be any hurtful way in me, and lead me in the everlasting way."

Assignment

1. This week when you are feeling guilty about something, confront it and repent if necessary.

2. Read chapter 6 of the text and work through the corresponding study.

CHAPTER SIX

CHOOSING RELAXATION OVER STRESS

Session Topic: Having an attitude of relaxation instead of an attitude of stress will result in a response of expectation instead of panic.

Icebreakers *(Choose one)*

1. Do you or does anyone you know take one of the top-selling drugs today, Tagamet, Valium, or Inderal? What might this say about that person's life-style and attitude choices?

2. When stressful situations enter your life, what works for you in alleviating that stress?

Group Discussion Questions

1. Is stress always harmful? What are the characteristics of stress that make it harmful?

2. Why might God allow stressful situations in our lives? Consider James 1:2-4. Are trials the same as stress?

3. What does the author mean when he says that "lack of purpose in life causes a person to be a victim, rather than a shaper, of circumstances"?

4. Many of us complain that we are too busy. To what can we attribute our overloaded lifestyles? Can it be helped?

5. What are some strategies to effectively deal with unresolved anger?

6. How would you define materialism? In what ways does materialism cause stress?

7. What are the author's five suggestions for developing an attitude of relaxation? Can you think of any more?

Personal Application Questions

1. Is following Jesus Christ a cure for stress or a cause of stress in your life? Read Matthew 11:28-30. If you are stressed from your Christian life, pray that God will reveal His way of rest to you.

2. When you encounter "various trials" what is your first response? Is it possible to "consider it all joy"? (James 1:2-4) What helps you to choose relaxation over stress in these situations?

3. As you think of your current stress-producers, could any of them be based on unrealistic goals or expectations? Do you have a way to determine if something is unrealistic for you? How would this tie in with choosing perseverance over defeat?

4. Is comparison a cause of stress for you? What things do you tend to compare? How can you choose relaxation in this instance?

5. Living life in the present tense is difficult for many people. Do you tend to be more stressed about the past or about the future?

6. Do you practice or desire a day of rest? What would your ideal day of rest be like? Is it possible?

7. Are you able to spend relaxed time with God each day? Why or why not? Where does your stress in this area come from? How can you respond correctly to that stress?

Optional Activities

1. At the end of one day this week, write down everything that you believe caused you stress that day. Consider each item and see if you can determine the root cause and a way you could have chosen an attitude of relaxation in response to it.

2. Copy Matthew 11:28-30 onto a note card and carry it around with you. When stress hits, read the card and pray for God's rest.

Prayer Focus

Thank God that His yoke is easy and his load is light. Thank God for His invitation to come to Him when you are weary and heavy-laden and for the promise that He will give you rest. Ask Him to help you do things that will allow strength, tranquility, and relaxation to mark your life.

Assignment

1. Make a point to take control of your attitude during stressful moments and remind yourself of God's perspective on it all.

2. Read chapter 7 of the text and work through the corresponding study.

CHAPTER SEVEN

CHOOSING CONTENTMENT OVER COMPARISON

Session Topic: Our relationship with Christ is a resource that enables us to choose contentment regardless of the circumstances.

Icebreaker *(Choose one)*

1. Describe someone you know who comes closest to living his or her life in contentment.
2. Imagine this scenario. A woman is very happy living with her family in a decent apartment. She visits a friend who is at her same life stage. Her friend's house is large and attractively furnished. What are the two women thinking and feeling about this difference?

Group Discovery Questions

1. Benjamin Franklin said "Who is rich? He that is content. Who is that? Nobody?" Do you agree? Why?
2. How does comparison steal our happiness?
3. What is the difference between observation, appreciation, desire to excel, and comparison?
4. The author describes covetousness as "the climax of the decalogue" and says that violations of the first nine commandments are "the natural by-products of dissatisfaction that stems from comparison." Do you think comparison is that serious? Try to come up with an example of how this assertion might be true for each commandment.
5. Is all investing based on the desire for more? Can a desire for more ever be based on something besides greed?
6. Explain how the love of money is a root of all sorts of evil. What is our proper relationship to money?
7. The author says "Paul was always content with what he had, but never with what he was." Is this what we should strive for? What was Paul's secret? (Philippians 4:11-13)

Personal Application Questions

1. In what area of your life is comparison the biggest problem?

2. Complete this sentence, "I could be really happy if only I had _____."

3. What is your attitude toward money? Does it ever divert your attention from God? Are you content with the money you have?

4. How can you prevent the Jeffress' Law from being true in your life? "Expenses expand to fill the available income."

5. When you are content, to what do you attribute this attitude? Have you ever successfully chosen contentment over comparison? If so, what motivated this choice?

6. Can you say of yourself that all that matters is God's approval? Can you say that your standard of success is knowing the will of God and doing it?

7. The author relates the story of the man who was angry because he didn't get his daily free $100 bill. Have you ever been in a similar position as either the giver or the receiver? What expectations can we truly have of God?

Optional Activities

1. Do a role-play of Icebreaker #2. Instruct two volunteers to say what the woman really might say in that situation and then to say "she would be thinking. . . . " Discuss what would be a godly response to the situation.

2. Write a list of your basic expectations in life. Prayerfully examine them. Should your list be shortened? Imagine that one or more of these expectations will not be met. How does this affect your relationship with God?

Prayer Focus

Pray that God will set your expectations and that you will be thankful for and content with what you are given. Confess attitudes of comparison. Ask God for strength to choose an attitude of contentment for each day.

Assignment

1. Be alert to your attitudes of comparison this week and strive to choose contentment in their place.

2. Read chapter 8 of the text and work through the corresponding study.

CHAPTER EIGHT

CHOOSING FORGIVENESS
OVER BITTERNESS

Session Topic: On the basis of God's forgiveness of us, we should choose to forgive by acknowledging and dismissing the offense instead of bitterly holding on to it.

Icebreaker *(Choose one)*
1. Describe a movie or television show which demonstrates the destructive effects of bitterness.
2. When did you first understand and believe that God forgives you on the basis of grace and not works?

Group Discovery Questions
1. How would you define forgiveness and bitterness?
2. Are there instances in which it would be better to not forgive? How can we continually forgive people and not just be inviting their abuse of us?
3. What is the proper response when someone offends you by gossip? By direct verbal rudeness? By deliberate deceit?
4. In your experience, do some people seem to deserve forgiveness and some not? If so, what is the difference between those two groups? Does that influence your attitude choice? Should it?
5. Why do you guess God makes forgiveness a matter of grace instead of works?
6. How did Joseph avoid bitterness toward his brothers?
7. In what way does choosing forgiveness relate to our eternal destiny? (Matthew 5:12-15)

Personal Application Questions
1. What is one example, past or present, of bitterness in your life? In what way did you choose to hold on to the offense?
2. Think of a situation in which the other person really did not deserve to be forgiven. Were you able to forgive that person? If so, how did you do it?
3. Have you ever chosen to not forgive because you felt it

was the best thing to do given the situation? Explain.

4. Can you look at a past offense in your life and exclaim with Joseph that "you meant evil against me, but God meant it for good"?

5. How do you presently feel toward the mistakes your parents made while raising you? What would show you that you have truly forgiven them?

6. Complete the exercise suggested by the author examining the six categories where you may need to exercise forgiveness. What is difficult for you about this exercise?

7. The author reminds us that all things that happen in our lives "are being used by God to mold you into the image of Christ." Do you view your life this way? How about the lives of Christian friends or family members? How would you apply this as you counsel a friend who has cancer, as you help a pregnant teenager, or as you advise someone who has come upon sudden financial wealth?

Optional Activities

1. Break into groups of two or three. Share one situation in which you are finding it difficult to forgive. Commit to one concrete action toward forgiveness. Pray for each other.

2. Look up the words *forgive/forgiveness* and *bitter/ bitterness* in your Bible concordance, and divide the verses up so you can read some each day for the next week. Choose one to memorize.

Prayer Focus

Praise God for forgiving your great debt when you did not deserve anything, and ask Him to help you choose the attitude of forgiveness toward others.

Assignment

1. As hurts come your way this week, ask yourself "How is God using this to conform me to the image of His Son?" You may want to place this question as a reminder to you on your desk at work, by your phone, or wherever you'll need it most. In this way you can cooperate with God's work in your life.

2. Read chapter 9 of the text and work through the corresponding study.

CHAPTER NINE

CHOOSING PRODUCTIVITY OVER LAZINESS

Session Topic: We should choose an attitude of productivity and harness the resources God has given us instead of wasting those gifts through an attitude of laziness.

Icebreakers *(Choose one)*

1. Has a new product ever come out that you had already thought of? What stopped you from pursuing your idea?
2. Proverbs 24:32 talks about someone learning a lesson from what he saw. What is something that you have observed that has taught you a lesson about choosing an attitude of productivity over laziness?

Group Discovery Questions

1. Consider one of the author's questions "Does the Bible promise riches?" What do you think? What is your view based on?
2. How are faith and material prosperity related?
3. What are some characteristics of a sluggard?
4. In what ways can greed harm a person? (See Luke 12:15-21.)
5. Is it possible for Christians to do too much while trying to maximize what God has given them? If so, how could you know what is enough and what is too much?
6. What would you say are the priorities of an average non-Christian as you look at their areas or goals of productivity? What about members in your church? What about your own family and your own life?

Personal Application Questions

1. Have you ever lost an opportunity because of laziness? Explain.
2. How does your theology concerning faith and prosperity affect your lifestyle? Are there any changes you should make?
3. As you read about the sluggard, who were you thinking about? How did you rate yourself?
4. In what area would "five minutes more" make a difference for you?

5. How would you rank the following priorities in your life: making money, being successful in business, spending time with family and friends, serving God? Are your efforts directed in this way?

6. Assuming some of these choices are learned, how can parents encourage their children to get in the practice of choosing productivity over laziness?

Optional Activities

1. The author says that productivity and laziness are examples of "mental and emotional responses to the circumstances of life." Role play the following circumstances by responding first with an attitude of laziness and then with an attitude of productivity.

a. Making good grades comes easy to you and you can finish your work with time to spare in class. What will happen in that last 15 minutes of each class?

b. It is Saturday and new neighbors just moved in. What is your response?

c. Each month you earn just a little bit more money than you need for your living expenses. What will you do with it?

2. Write down what you would have done differently yesterday if you had constantly asked yourself the question "What is the most productive thing I could be doing *now?*"

Prayer Focus

Thank God for the time, resources, and talents that He has given you and ask Him to help you continue to choose an attitude of productivity for His glory and service.

Assignment

1. Before you go to bed each night this week, write down the six most important things you can accomplish the next day.

2. Read chapter 10 of the text and work through the corresponding study.

CHAPTER TEN

CHOOSING HUMILITY OVER PRIDE

Session Topic: As you experience successes and failures, choose to have God's perspective and humbly give credit where it is truly due.

Icebreakers *(Choose one)*

1. Suppose a Christian has trained hard for an athletic event and then proceeds to win it. After the victory, a reporter asks "To what do you attribute this great success?" How should the athlete respond?

2. The phrase "I put my foot in my mouth" describes a time when one has made a statement which resulted in embarrassment and a dose of humility. Tell of such an incident from your own life.

Group Discovery Questions

1. How would you define pride?

2. Modern psychology targets the lack of self-esteem as a root cause for the problems of many people. The Bible has much to say about people thinking *too* highly of themselves. Can these both be true? If so, how? If not, where has the false view gone wrong?

3. With regard to independence and feeling no need for God, compare people throughout history (e.g. people of the Exodus, of Jesus' era, the early centuries after Christ, the early 20th century, 1960-70, 1980-present). Is the problem of pride in general always the same, getting better, or getting worse?

4. Share the worst example of racism that you have seen, heard of, or experienced. What do you think is the cause of racism? What is the antidote?

5. Do you agree that the inability to accept God's forgiveness is because of pride? Is that a new thought to you? If so, what has been your understanding in the past?

6. What does Romans 1:18-32 have to say about pride? How are our great universities doing in regard to the phrase "although they claimed to be wise, they became fools"?

7. What is the key to doing your best and not being concerned who gets the credit?

Personal Application Questions
1. Think of one success and one failure in your life. How did you react to each?
2. Write down 8-10 of the best things in your life. Are any of these a source of pride for you in that you have been giving yourself all the credit? Take a moment to give thanks to God. Express that thanks in a public way also.
3. Which good gift in your life gives you the most trouble in remembering the Giver?
4. How do pride and ingratitude affect your personal relationship to God? Confess this now.
5. When involved in a disagreement, how willing are you to admit that you may not be right? What are some steps you can take to improve in that area?
6. What is God's perspective of your worth and capabilities?

Optional Activities
1. Study the following passages and look for examples of pride and humility in the Apostle Paul: 2 Corinthians 11:5–12:10; Philippians 3:3-10; Ephesians 3:8; 4:1.
2. Visit a planetarium during the week and ponder on the greatness of God's creation and your part in it all.

Prayer Focus
Thank God for all the good gifts he has given you. Confess general attitudes as well as specific instances of your pride, independence, ingratitude. Ask Him to help you to learn true humility.

Assignment
1. Read chapter 11 of the text and work through the corresponding study.
2. Each day run a mental check on your attitudes toward other people that you encountered. Keep a lookout for pride (through comparison, independence, ingratitude, intolerance) and when you find it, replace that prideful attitude with an attitude of humility.

CHAPTER ELEVEN

CHOOSING COMPANIONSHIP OVER LONELINESS

Session Topic: Put off self-sufficiency and choose instead the companionship attitude which includes others as necessary for your emotional and spiritual health.

Icebreakers *(Choose one)*
1. If you were stranded on a desert island and could choose one person to be marooned with, who would you choose and why?
2. If the fire in the fireplace is great Christian fellowship and the cold floor is loneliness and isolation, where would you place yourself as a log: red hot, red, orange, gray, or cold black?

Group Discovery Questions
1. What was your first reaction to the idea that loneliness is an attitude choice? Do you have difficulty in fully accepting this idea? If so, why?
2. What is the cure for a poor self-image? How can a person make sure that a good self-image doesn't develop into pride?
3. Read Matthew 5:23-24 and Matthew 18:15. In what instances should you be the one to initiate reconciliation with a fellow Christian?
4. Does it matter if a Christian finds his or her companionship with unbelievers? What is dangerous about not being closely involved with other Christians?
5. Do you think most Christians want accountability? Why or why not?
6. Is it possible for a spouse to satisfy all of a person's needs for companionship? What role do friends play in a married person's life? What role do friends play in a single person's life?

Personal Application Questions
1. In the joys and sorrows of life, do you choose to go it alone or invite companionship?

2. If and when you choose to be lonely, what is the most likely reason? How does this period usually end?

3. How might busyness actually be selfishness in your life? Are there any activities or commitments that you can eliminate in order to be less busy and more available?

4. Has an unwillingness to forgive a friend or family member caused you to be alienated from them? What steps can you take to make things right?

5. Does companionship seem to make a difference in your physical, emotional and/or spiritual health? Is there anyone in your family that seems to be affected by an abundance or a lack of companionship?

6. Was there a time when you received one or more of the four benefits of a companionship (assistance in times of crises, support when we feel alone, protection when we are under siege, accountability when we are prone to waver)? What is your most fulfilling example of being on the helping end?

Optional Activities

1. Draw a graph of your life with the peaks being high points of companionship and the valleys being low points of loneliness. Share this with the group or a friend.

2. Sing together a companionship song such as "Bind Us Together" or "We are One in the Spirit." Hold hands in a circle if it is appropriate.

Prayer Focus

Thank God for all the companions you have been given throughout your life. Ask God to help you when you are feeling lonely and blue to choose companionship and to be willing to be someone else's companion.

Assignment

1. Next Sunday in your church service, notice who is sitting together and who is sitting alone. Make a point to reach out to those who might be lonely.

2. Read chapter 12 of the text and work through the corresponding study.

CHAPTER TWELVE

CHOOSING INTIMACY WITH GOD OVER ISOLATION

Session Topic: Choosing to develop an intimate relationship with God is life's most important attitude choice.

Icebreakers *(Choose one)*
1. Relate your most memorable travel story in which you got lost. Would a good map have helped?
2. Have you ever kept a journal? How long did you keep it, and how do you feel about it now?

Group Discovery Questions
1. How would you describe intimacy with God? What would a person be like who had chosen to live in this intimacy with God?
2. Think of someone you know who has tried (or is currently trying) one or more of the "maps" that Solomon tried—pleasure, wisdom, or work. Did these directions in life seem to prove worthwhile?
3. Which of the above wrong "maps" do you think is the greatest temptation to American Christians today?
4. The author's father had worked and saved for his old age and didn't live to enjoy it. What is the proper way to live our lives in light of Matthew 6:33-34?
5. How would a person's life be different if he or she chose to view life from under the sun as compared to above the sun?
6. How does this attitude choice work as the foundation for the other eleven listed by the author?

Personal Application Questions
1. Which of the three wrong maps (pleasure, wisdom, work) has the most allure for you? How can you prevent these directions of life from distracting you from putting God first?
2. Step #2 for developing intimacy with God is to "Honestly evaluate your relationship with God." Read Colossians 3:1-2. How are you doing?

3. Do you need to repent and change direction in any area? If so, do so today. If not, recall a time when you recommitted yourself to intimacy with God as a first priority and resolve again to continue in this choice.

4. Do you tend to depend on someone or something other than God to satisfy your deepest needs? How can you rearrange that priority?

5. How does it affect you when you skip prayer and Bible reading for two or more days? What motivates you to get back on track?

6. On which of the 11 attitude choices described by the author, do you feel it is most essential that you make improvements? Share this with one other person and ask them to keep a check on you for accountability.

Optional Activities

1. Take a quiet moment to reflect on a problem you are currently experiencing. Imagine yourself on an airplane runway with the weather gray, cold, and rainy. Think of your problem from this viewpoint of "under the sun." Now imagine looking out the window as the plane takes off and rises higher and higher. Suddenly you break through the clouds and are out in the bright blue sky with the beautiful sunshine flooding your soul. Now consider your problem from "above the sun." Ask God for this higher perspective.

2. Survey several Christians from your local church with these two questions: "What is the biggest hindrance to your nurturing your relationship with Christ in the way you should? What helps you the most in the nurturing of your relationship with Christ?

Prayer Focus

Thank God for the many insights and challenges He has brought to you through this study. Ask Him to help you to make the choices of attitude that are pleasing in His sight.

CHAPTER ONE: Attitude Is Everything
1. John Haggai, cited in *Eating Problems for Breakfast* by Tim Hansel (Waco, Texas: Word, Inc., 1988), 28-29.
2. Frank B. Minirth and Paul D. Meier, *Happiness Is a Choice* (Grand Rapids, Michigan: Baker Book House, 1978), 133.
3. Dennis Waitley, *Seeds of Greatness* (Old Tappan, New Jersey: Fleming H. Revell Company, 1983), 51.

CHAPTER TWO: Choosing Purpose over Aimlessness
1. Charles Colson, *Kingdoms in Conflict* (A copublication of William Morrow and Zondervan Publishing House, 1987), 68.
2. Bobb Biehl, *Masterplan Your Life in One Day* (Laguna Niguel, California: Masterplanning Group, International, 1985), 6.
3. Ibid.
4. Ibid., 3.

CHAPTER THREE: Choosing Perseverance over Defeat
1. Tim Hansel, *Eating Problems for Breakfast* (Waco, Texas: Word, Inc., 1988), 118-19.
2. Source unknown.
3. Dr. David Wechsler, cited in *Motivation to Last a Lifetime* by Ted W. Engstrom (Grand Rapids, Michigan: Zondervan Publishing House, 1984), 40.
4. Napoleon Hill, *Think and Grow Rich* (New York: Ballantine Books, 1983), 164.
5. Engstrom, *Motivation*, 76.
6. Thomas Watson statement: Roger von Oech, *A Whack on the Side of the Head* (New York: Warner Books, Inc., 1983), 93.
7. Edwin C. Bliss, cited in *Be All You Can Be!* by John C. Maxwell, (Wheaton, Illinois: Victor Books, 1987), 108-9.
8. Dennis Waitley, *Seeds of Greatness* (Old Tappan, New Jersey: Fleming H. Revell Company, 1983), 88.

9. Amy Carmichael, cited in *Holy Sweat* by Tim Hansel (Waco, Texas: Word, Inc., 1988), 130.

CHAPTER FOUR: Choosing Faith over Worry
1. Lloyd M. Perry and Charles M. Sell, *Speaking to Life's Problems* (Chicago: Moody Press, 1983), 161-62.
2. Charles Swindoll, in his weekly column, *Think It Over*, published by the First Evangelical Free Church of Fullerton, California. Date unknown.
3. Warren W. Wiersbe, *Be Joyful* (Wheaton, Illinois: Victor Books, 1974), 129.

CHAPTER FIVE: Choosing Repentance over Guilt
1. Source unknown.
2. Norman Cousins, *Head First: The Biology of Hope* (New York: E.P. Dutton, 1989), 109.
3. Frank B. Minirth and Paul D. Meier, *Happiness Is a Choice* (Grand Rapids, Michigan: Baker Book House, 1978), 70.

CHAPTER SIX: Choosing Relaxation over Stress
1. Lloyd J. Ogilvie, *Making Stress Work for You* (Waco, Texas: Word, Inc., 1984), 21.
2. John MacArthur, Jr., *1 Corinthians: MacArthur New Testament Commentary* (Chicago: Moody Press, 1984), 448.
3. Rita Rubin, "Responses to stress influences ability to fight off illness," *The Dallas Morning News*, 12 March 1990, 7D.
4. Norman Cousins, *Head First: The Biology of Hope* (New York: E.P. Dutton, 1989), 300.
5. Ibid., 86.
6. Rita Rubin, "Responses to stress influences ability to fight off illness," *The Dallas Morning News*, 12 March 1990, 7D.
7. Tim Hansel, *When I Relax I Feel Guilty* (Elgin, Illinois: David C. Cook Publishing Co., 1979), 110-11.
8. Frank B. Minirth and Paul D. Meier, *Happiness Is a Choice* (Grand Rapids, Michigan: Baker Book House, 1978), 113.

9. Helen Mallicoat, cited in *Holy Sweat* by Tim Hansel (Waco, Texas: Word, Inc., 1987), 136.
10. Gordon MacDonald, *Ordering Your Private World* (Nashville, Tennessee: Oliver-Nelson, 1984), 184.
11. Garth Lean, cited in *Ordering Your Private World* by Gordon MacDonald, 174.
12. Harvey Mackay, *Beware the Naked Man Who Offers You His Shirt* (New York: William Morrow and Company, Inc., 1990), 157.

CHAPTER SEVEN: Choosing Contentment over Comparison
1. Robert Jeffress, *Faith at the Crossroads* (Nashville: Broadman Press, 1989), 113.
2. Ann Landers, March 20, 1989. Permission granted by Ann Landers and Creators Syndicate.
3. Some of the ideas in this section are adapted from chapter 12 of my book *Faith at the Crossroads*.

CHAPTER EIGHT: Choosing Forgiveness over Bitterness
1. Ann Landers, August 15, 1990. Permission granted by Ann Landers and Creators Syndicate.
2. Jan Hindman, *Just before Dawn* (Ontario, Oregon: Alexandria Associates, 1989), 418-20.

CHAPTER NINE: Choosing Productivity over Laziness
1. Robert Tilton, cited in *The Agony of Deceit* edited by Michael Horton (Chicago: Moody Press, 1990), 276.
2. Derek Kidner, *Proverbs* (Downers Grove, Illinois: InterVarsity Press, 1964), 43.
3. Ted W. Engstrom, *The Pursuit of Excellence* (Grand Rapids, Michigan: Zondervan Publishing House, 1982), 33.
4. Ibid., 33-34.
5. Gordon MacDonald, *Ordering Your Private World* (Nashville, Tennessee: Oliver-Nelson, 1984), 70.
6. R. Alec Mackenzie, *The Time Trap* (New York: McGraw-Hill Book Company, 1972), 38-39.
7. John D. Morgan, *Financial Freedom Syllabus*, 1978, 6.
8. John MacArthur, Jr., Word of Grace Communications, February, 1987.

9. Harold Kushner, *When All You've Ever Wanted Isn't Enough* (New York: Pocket Books, a division of Simon and Schuster, Inc., 1986), 15-16.

CHAPTER TEN: Choosing Humility over Pride
1. Ted W. Engstrom, *The Fine Art of Mentoring* (Brentwood, Tennessee: Wolgemuth and Hyatt, Inc., 1989), 81-82.

CHAPTER ELEVEN: Choosing Companionship over Loneliness
1. Lloyd M. Perry and Charles M. Sell, *Speaking to Life's Problems* (Chicago: Moody Press, 1983), 205.
2. Ibid., 206-7.
3. Frederick W. Robertson, cited in *Speaking to Life's Problems*, 207.
4. Jerry and Mary White, *Friends and Friendship* (Colorado Springs: NavPress, 1982), 25.
5. *Modern Maturity* (February-March, 1990), 18-19.
6. Several ideas in this section are adapted from *Living on the Ragged Edge* by Charles R. Swindoll (Waco, Texas: Word, Inc., 1985), 134-38.
7. White, *Friends and Friendship*, 33-38.
8. Harold Kushner, *When All You've Ever Wanted Isn't Enough* (New York: Pocket Books, a division of Simon and Schuster, Inc., 1986), 53.

CHAPTER TWELVE: Choosing Intimacy with God over Isolation
1. Steven R. Covey, *The Seven Habits of Highly Effective People* (New York: Simon and Schuster, Inc., 1989), 23-24.
2. Walker C. Kaiser, Jr., *Ecclesiastes: Total Life* (Chicago: Moody Press, 1979), 118.